Overcoming Obstacles

Resilience Techniques from the World's Most Successful

Author – Stan Barren

Brought to you by InspirationDB

Stan Barren

Legal and Copyright Disclaimer

Exclusive Offer Inside!

Have you ever found yourself questioning the direction of your life or wondering if there's more to your journey? We have something special just for you - a roadmap to finding that missing piece, a guide to uncovering the purpose that fuels your passion and drives your ambitions.

Introducing "The Ultimate Guide to Finding Your Life's Purpose."

Whether you're at a crossroads, feeling lost, or simply curious about what makes life truly meaningful, this comprehensive e-book has the insights, exercises, and stories to illuminate your path.

And here's the best part: We're giving it away for FREE! Don't miss out! Subscribe to our email newsletter now and get instant access to "The Ultimate Guide to Finding Your Life's Purpose." Discover the passion, meaning, and drive that's waiting within you.

Get now from InspirationDB.com/FREE

Stan Barren

Table of Contents

Introduction

In every life, rain must fall. Whether we're faced with personal struggles, professional setbacks, or the myriad challenges that are part and parcel of the human experience, obstacles are an inevitable part of our journey.

But while we can't always control the challenges that confront us, we can determine our response to them. It is in this interplay between adversity and response that the concept of resilience finds its true significance.

The world is replete with stories of individuals who have faced insurmountable odds, only to emerge stronger, wiser, and more successful. These individuals, both from history and contemporary times, serve as beacons of hope, illuminating the path for those of us grappling with our own challenges.

Their stories are not just testaments to the indomitable human spirit but also provide practical lessons on how to navigate life's tumultuous seas.

"Overcoming Obstacles: Resilience Techniques from the World's Most Successful" seeks to delve deep into the strategies and mindsets adopted by these high achievers, unearthing the secrets behind their resilience.

Whether it's the tale of a business magnate who faced repeated failures before finding success or an artist who struggled against societal norms to create masterpieces, these narratives hold invaluable insights.

But this book is not just about tales of triumph. It's a toolkit, a guidebook, a mentor in print. By exploring the psychology of resilience, examining the role of mindset, and providing practical tools and techniques, this book aims to empower its readers.

The goal is not just to inspire but to equip you with actionable strategies to face and overcome your challenges.

As you turn the pages, remember that every chapter, every anecdote, every piece of advice stem from a place of understanding. We all face obstacles.

Yet, it's not the size of the challenge but the strength of our response that truly defines us. Embark on this journey not just as a reader, but as an individual committed to embracing challenges, learning from them, and emerging resilient.

Welcome to a voyage of discovery, reflection, and empowerment. Welcome to "Overcoming Obstacles."

The Universality of Obstacles and Challenges

Obstacles and challenges are an inherent part of the human experience, spanning across time, cultures, geographies, and individual life paths. No matter one's socio-economic status, geographic location, age, or background, everyone, at some point or another, confronts hurdles they must overcome.

It's a uniting thread in the tapestry of life that interweaves kings with commoners, the affluent with the underprivileged, and the young with the old.

Historical records and ancient texts, ranging from epics like the Mahabharata, the Iliad, or the works of Shakespeare, often centralize the theme of adversity.

They serve as testaments to the age-old nature of challenges, emphasizing that obstacles aren't just a modern-day phenomenon but have been present since the dawn of human civilization. From ancient emperors managing the intricacies of kingdoms to farmers trying to predict and survive the wrath of nature, challenges have persistently been the norm.

Furthermore, the universality of obstacles is not confined merely to an individual level. Entire communities, nations, and civilizations have faced adversities.

Historical events such as wars, famines, economic depressions, and pandemics have affected vast swathes of populations, underlining the collective aspect of challenges. Yet, as much as these events have tested the mettle of humanity, they have also fostered unity, resilience, and innovation.

It's also noteworthy to reflect upon personal life stages, from childhood to old age. A child grapples with learning new skills, a teenager might struggle with identity and acceptance, adults often face challenges related to work, relationships, and health, while the elderly might find it hard to cope with aging and the loss of peers. These stages emphasize that challenges are not discriminatory; they are an inevitable part of life's journey.

In essence, understanding the universality of obstacles offers two vital perspectives. First, it provides solace in knowing that one is not alone in their struggles; challenges are a shared human experience. Second, it presents an opportunity: since time immemorial, individuals and communities have not only faced but often thrived in the wake of challenges.

This resilience and ability to transform adversity into opportunity is a hallmark of the human spirit, offering hope and inspiration for anyone navigating life's many hurdles.

The Importance of Resilience in Overcoming Challenges

Resilience is often likened to a rubber band's ability to snap back to its original form after being stretched. In the human context, it is our innate ability to bounce back from adversities, traumas, and hardships. In life, challenges are inevitable.

From personal hurdles like illness or job loss to larger societal issues such as economic downturns or natural disasters, we all face setbacks. However, it is resilience that often determines whether we are defeated by these challenges or whether we rise from them stronger and more equipped for the future.

At its core, resilience is not just about returning to our former state after a setback, but about undergoing positive adaptation and growth as a result. This "post-traumatic growth" can lead individuals to develop new insights, re-evaluate their priorities, and often discover a deeper sense of purpose.

It fosters a mentality that sees challenges not as insurmountable threats, but as opportunities for growth and development. Thus, instead of being overwhelmed, resilient individuals utilize challenges to mold themselves, learning lessons, building inner strength, and often emerging with a more nuanced perspective on life.

Moreover, resilience is closely associated with a plethora of positive psychological and physiological outcomes. Psychologically, resilient individuals tend to exhibit lower levels of depression, better overall mental health, and higher life satisfaction. They possess coping strategies that allow them to navigate the intricacies of emotional distress with greater ease.

Physiologically, resilience can lead to better cardiovascular health, a more robust immune system, and even increased longevity. These benefits are linked to the reduced chronic stress experienced by those who can adapt and recover swiftly from adversities.

In a rapidly changing world, where uncertainties and challenges have become the norm, resilience acts as an invaluable shield. It buffers against the mental health toll that repeated setbacks can inflict and offers a pathway to not just survival, but thriving.

Without resilience, every setback has the potential to be a breaking point. But with it, each challenge is just another stepping stone, contributing to a journey of continuous growth and transformation. In essence, resilience doesn't just help us survive the storms of life, but teaches us how to dance in the rain.

A Brief Overview of What the Book Will Cover

In "Overcoming Obstacles: Resilience Techniques from the World's Most Successful", we embark on a profound journey, delving deep into the tumultuous seas of challenges that have been faced and overcome by both historical and contemporary figures.

From the societal restraints battled by leaders like Nelson Mandela to the personal demons wrestled by figures such as Winston Churchill, this book unravels the intricate tapestry of resilience woven by individuals from varied walks of life.

The very fabric of this book is designed to offer readers an understanding of the nature of obstacles, both internal and external. It aims to dissect the psychology that underpins resilience and the mindset shifts essential for one to rise above adversity.

The narrative isn't just historical; it's also refreshingly contemporary, with stories of modern titans from diverse sectors, business, sports, and entertainment. Figures like Elon Musk and Serena Williams take center stage, illuminating the path with their tales of perseverance.

But this book isn't just about stories. It's also a practical guide. We venture into the world of actionable strategies, drawing from both time-tested wisdom and cutting-edge research.

Readers will be equipped with mental conditioning exercises, introduced to the transformative power of self-care, and shown the significance of a strong support system. Moreover, the narrative delves into the often-overlooked aspect of failure, portraying it not as a pitfall but as a stepping stone to greater heights.

Furthermore, in a world increasingly dominated by technology, our book also bridges the gap between age-old resilience techniques and modern tools. From meditation apps to journaling exercises, readers will be introduced to a plethora of resources to bolster their resilience arsenal.

Concluding with a forward-looking perspective, "Overcoming Obstacles" doesn't just prepare readers for the challenges of today but also for the uncertainties of tomorrow. By the end of this journey, readers won't merely understand resilience; they'll be imbued with it, ready to face life's trials with newfound vigor and determination.

Chapter 1: The Nature of Obstacles

Obstacles. We've all faced them. From the moment we took our first step, uttered our first word, or tried something new, we were met with challenges that shaped our journey.

Whether they manifest as boulders blocking our path or as subtle internal whispers of doubt, these obstacles play a pivotal role in our life story. But what exactly constitutes an obstacle? Is it merely a physical barrier, or can it be something more intangible?

In this chapter, we will delve deep into understanding the very nature of obstacles. We'll differentiate between the external hurdles, the ones that the world throws at us, and the internal challenges, the fears, insecurities, and doubts that arise from within.

Throughout history, both types of obstacles have tested the mettle of individuals, pushing them to either rise above or falter. As we explore the intricacies of these challenges, we'll also touch upon how different eras and cultures perceive obstacles and how their definitions and significances have evolved over time.

By the end of this chapter, you'll have a comprehensive understanding of the multifaceted nature of obstacles. This foundational knowledge will serve as a stepping stone, allowing you to better appreciate the resilience techniques discussed in the subsequent chapters.

Let's embark on this journey together, understanding that every challenge we face offers us an opportunity for growth.

Defining obstacles: Internal vs. External

At some point in our lives, each of us faces hurdles that challenge our status quo, testing our patience, resilience, and spirit. These obstacles can vary significantly in nature, intensity, and impact. Broadly speaking, they can be categorized into two primary types: internal and external.

Internal Obstacles

Internal obstacles are challenges that originate within us and often stem from our thoughts, emotions, and beliefs. They are the mental barriers and psychological hurdles that prevent us from taking action, making decisions, or realizing our potential. Self-doubt, fear, limiting beliefs, lack of motivation, perfectionism, procrastination, and low self-esteem are common examples.

For instance, someone may have the capability to start a new business venture but might hold back due to a deep-seated fear of failure or the belief that they aren't "entrepreneur material." Such beliefs and fears aren't necessarily rooted in reality but are powerful enough to prevent one from pursuing their goals.

Often, these internal obstacles are products of past experiences, cultural conditioning, or negative influences from early life. Overcoming these challenges requires introspection, self-awareness, and often a commitment to personal growth and mental well-being.

External Obstacles

In contrast, external obstacles are challenges that arise from the environment and situations around us. They aren't directly linked to our personal feelings or beliefs but are often circumstances we have little control over.

Examples include economic downturns, physical disabilities, societal prejudices, family responsibilities, or geographical constraints.

Take, for instance, an aspiring athlete who has the talent and determination to excel in their sport but is held back due to a lack of necessary training facilities in their hometown. Or consider someone who has the skills for a job but faces discrimination because of their background or appearance.

These are situations where external factors limit one's progress. Tackling external obstacles often demands a combination of strategic planning, resourcefulness, and sometimes, advocacy for broader change.

In essence, while both internal and external obstacles pose challenges, the strategies to overcome them can differ significantly. Recognizing the nature of the obstacle is the first step in devising an effective solution.

Whether the challenge is within our minds or in the world around us, understanding its root cause can illuminate the path forward.

Historical Context: Famous Figures and the Challenges They Faced

Frida Kahlo: The iconic Mexican painter faced numerous adversities in her life. At the age of 18, she was severely injured in a bus accident, leading to long-term physical pain and medical complications.

This pain often manifested in her vivid and surrealistic artwork. Moreover, her tumultuous relationship with the famed muralist Diego Rivera, coupled with her inability to have children, often left her emotionally distraught.

Despite these challenges, or perhaps because of them, Kahlo's work resonated with deep emotional authenticity, making her one of the most celebrated artists of the 20th century.

Her life serves as a testament to the strength of the human spirit in the face of physical and emotional adversity.

Marie Curie: A pioneering scientist, Curie faced the double-edged sword of gender biases and the perils of her ground-breaking work. She became the first woman to win a Nobel Prize and remains the only person to have won Nobel Prizes in two different scientific fields: Physics and Chemistry.

Yet, despite her ground-breaking work on radioactivity, she faced skepticism and prejudice in the male-dominated world of science.

Furthermore, her extensive exposure to radiation, a hazard unknown at the time, led to health issues that eventually caused her death.

Curie's dedication to science in the face of personal risk and societal doubt emphasizes the sacrifices some make in the pursuit of knowledge and progress.

Harriet Tubman: Born into slavery, Tubman escaped to freedom only to risk her life repeatedly by returning to the South to lead other slaves to freedom via the Underground Railroad.

Facing the constant danger of capture, punishment, or worse, she also dealt with health issues stemming from a childhood injury.

Tubman was not just a conductor on the Underground Railroad; she was also a spy for the Union during the Civil War and later became an advocate for women's suffrage.

Her life exemplifies the incredible feats one can achieve with sheer determination, bravery, and a deep-seated belief in justice and equality.

Oskar Schindler: A German industrialist during World War II, Schindler is renowned for his efforts to save over a thousand Jews from the Holocaust. Initially motivated by economic interests, his conscience gradually took precedence as he witnessed the brutalities of the Nazi regime.

Operating within a system that was inherently against his mission, Schindler utilized his connections, wits, and resources to protect his Jewish workers.

Despite facing financial ruin and significant personal risk, he persisted in his clandestine humanitarian effort. Schindler's story underscores the moral complexities individuals can face in times of widespread atrocity and the capacity for redemption and courage against overwhelming odds.

Rosa Parks: Often dubbed "the mother of the freedom movement," Rosa Parks ignited the Montgomery Bus Boycott when she refused to surrender her bus seat to a white passenger.

This act of defiance, seemingly simple yet profoundly brave, became a pivotal moment in the Civil Rights Movement. Parks faced arrest, professional repercussions, and threats to her life.

However, her quiet strength and unwavering resolve rallied a community and eventually a nation toward greater justice and equality. Parks' legacy reminds us of the profound impact that one individual's stand against injustice can have on the course of history.

Helen Keller: Born both deaf and blind, Helen Keller faced unimaginable obstacles from a very young age. However, with the support of her remarkable teacher, Anne Sullivan, Keller not only learned to communicate but also went on to become a world-famous speaker and author. She became an advocate for people with disabilities, women's suffrage, and worker's rights.

Her life story is a testament to the power of determination, education, and the human spirit to overcome even the most challenging of circumstances. Keller's journey reminds us that limitations are often only as restrictive as we allow them to be.

Leonardo da Vinci: Often heralded as the epitome of the Renaissance man, Leonardo faced illegitimacy in a society that heavily stigmatized it. This status barred him from formal education, such as attending a Latin school or university.

Yet, he turned this setback into an advantage, approaching knowledge with insatiable curiosity and without the confines of traditional schooling.

This self-directed education led him to achievements in art, science, engineering, anatomy, and many other fields. Leonardo's life underscores the idea that traditional paths aren't the only routes to success; sometimes, the most ground-breaking insights come from outside the established systems.

Joan of Arc: A peasant girl in medieval France, Joan of Arc rose to prominence when she believed she had visions from saints instructing her to support Charles VII and recover France from English domination.

Her conviction led her to play a key role in lifting the Siege of Orléans and ensuring Charles' coronation as the King of France.

However, her fortunes swiftly changed. Captured by the English, she faced trial and was eventually executed for charges including cross-dressing (she wore male military attire), heresy, and witchcraft.

Today, she's remembered not as a heretic but as a martyr and a symbol of courage and faith against overwhelming odds.

George Washington Carver: Born into slavery in the mid-1860s, Carver went on to become one of America's most prominent scientists and inventors.

With a deep passion for plants and a belief in the potential of alternative crops to aid impoverished farmers, he developed techniques to improve soils depleted by repeated plantings of cotton.

He introduced the idea of planting peanuts and sweet potatoes to restore nitrogen to the soil. Furthermore, Carver devised over 100 products using one major crop, the peanut, including dyes, plastics, and gasoline.

His journey, marked by perseverance and innovation, showcases the power of knowledge and passion to overcome systemic societal challenges.

Modern Day Examples: Common Obstacles in the 21st Century

Technological Overload: In the digital age, one of the primary challenges many faces is the inundation of technology in every aspect of life. While technology has enabled instantaneous communication, provided tools for innovation, and revolutionized industries, it has also brought about issues of digital dependency, decreased face-to-face social interactions, and concerns about data privacy.

The constant barrage of notifications, emails, and messages can be mentally exhausting, leading to burnout and decreased productivity. Additionally, the 'always-on' expectation in many workplaces has blurred the lines between professional and personal time, making work-life balance harder to achieve.

Mental Health Challenges: As the 21st century progresses, there's been a notable rise in mental health issues, particularly among younger generations. Factors like economic instability, academic pressures, social media comparison culture, and geopolitical uncertainties have contributed to heightened levels of stress, anxiety, and depression.

Though society is gradually destigmatizing mental health concerns, there's still a long way to go in terms of accessibility and affordability of care, as well as widespread understanding and support.

Environmental and Climate Crises: Modern society grapples with significant environmental challenges, from rampant deforestation to the alarming depletion of natural resources.

The consequences of climate change, including extreme weather events, rising sea levels, and shifting climate patterns, pose immediate and future threats to communities worldwide.

This looming ecological crisis not only impacts physical health and habitats but also brings about mental and emotional strain, as individuals and communities grapple with uncertain futures and the monumental task of environmental stewardship.

Economic Disparities: The widening gap between the rich and the poor is an acute obstacle of the modern era. Globalization and technological advancements have brought immense wealth to some, while others grapple with job losses due to automation and outsourcing.

Economic disparities are not just limited to income; they extend to access to quality education, healthcare, and opportunities, leading to systemic challenges that generations face.

Information Overload and Misinformation: The 21st century, with its vast digital landscapes, offers information at the fingertips. However, this abundance often leads to information overload, making it challenging to discern relevant data from the inconsequential.

Further complicating this is the spread of misinformation and fake news, which can rapidly disseminate through social media platforms and other online channels. Navigating this maze and cultivating a discerning, critical mindset has become an essential skill and challenge.

Chapter 2: Understanding Resilience

As we navigate the tumultuous waters of life, the concept of resilience often emerges as the buoy that keeps us afloat. It's a term that's easy to use but complex to define, layered with various shades of meaning and application.

Most of us recognize resilience when we see it, people who bounce back from setbacks, who seem unbreakable regardless of the challenges they face, who adapt and grow in the face of adversity. But what is this quality that seems so intangible, yet so crucial?

In this chapter, we'll demystify the concept of resilience, diving into its psychological underpinnings, its different dimensions, and its essential role in overcoming obstacles. We'll explore not only what resilience means, but also how it manifests in daily life and the profound impact it has on our ability to succeed.

Moreover, we will consider the facets of resilience that have been exhibited by some of the world's most successful people, looking to understand how this characteristic has contributed to their extraordinary achievements.

Understanding resilience is the first crucial step in developing it. By gaining a comprehensive understanding of this multifaceted trait, you'll be better equipped to face the inevitable challenges that life presents.

We'll examine the elements that make up resilience, the differences between innate and cultivated resilience, and why some people seem to have an abundant supply of this invaluable quality while others struggle to exhibit it.

So, let's embark on this illuminating journey together, dissecting the nature of resilience to equip you with the knowledge and insight necessary to fortify your own life against the obstacles ahead.

What Is Resilience?

Resilience: At its core, resilience refers to the capacity of an individual to withstand, adapt to, and recover from adversities, traumas, and significant sources of stress.

This might include family and relationship problems, serious health setbacks, or workplace and financial stressors. Rather than being disheartened by such challenges, those with resilience manage to find a way to rise from the ashes, often emerging even stronger than before.

In the realms of psychology and personal development, resilience doesn't merely mean "bouncing back" from these difficulties. It encompasses learning and personal growth that occurs as a result of the challenges faced.

This transformative aspect of resilience makes it distinct. It's about harnessing inner strength and external resources, and transforming adversity into an opportunity for growth.

Biologically speaking, resilience can be likened to the elasticity of a rubber band, stretching when faced with force but returning to its original state once the pressure is released.

For humans, however, resilience is more intricate. Our return to equilibrium after a challenge isn't just a passive rebound; it's often an active process that involves awareness, insight, and purposeful effort.

Several factors contribute to resilience. Personal characteristics like optimism, self-confidence, and a positive attitude undeniably play a role. But equally important are external factors, such as a supportive network of friends and family.

Skills like problem-solving, communication, and the ability to manage strong feelings and impulses also significantly bolster resilience.

Lastly, it's crucial to understand that resilience isn't a fixed trait or something people either have or don't have. It's malleable. With intention, awareness, and practice, individuals can cultivate and enhance their resilience throughout life.

This development often requires confronting and working through challenges, learning from experiences, and intentionally engaging in personal growth activities.

The Psychology Behind Resilient Individuals

Resilience, often described as the ability to bounce back from adversity and adapt in the face of challenging circumstances, is a trait not confined to a select few but is rather a blend of behaviors, thoughts, and actions that can be learned and developed.

The psychological makeup of resilient individuals reveals a combination of factors that enable them to navigate through life's harshest storms.

1. Positive Cognitive Appraisal: One of the hallmarks of resilient individuals is their ability to interpret challenges and adversities in a positive light. While they don't dismiss or minimize the gravity of a situation, they have a knack for seeing setbacks as temporary, specific, and external rather than permanent, pervasive, and internal.

This cognitive framing, often rooted in optimism, allows them to perceive difficulties as opportunities for growth rather than insurmountable problems.

2. Strong Sense of Self-efficacy: Resilient individuals harbor a deep-seated belief in their abilities to influence outcomes. Psychologist Albert Bandura referred to this as "self-efficacy", which is the conviction that one can successfully execute the behavior required to produce the desired outcomes.

It's this belief that instils a sense of agency and control, enabling resilient people to approach challenges with confidence, even when the odds are stacked against them.

3. Emotion Regulation: The capacity to manage and modulate emotional responses is crucial for resilience. Resilient individuals tend to be adept at using strategies that allow them to stay calm under pressure, manage anxiety, and maintain focus.

They are neither enslaved by their emotions nor dismissive of them; instead, they recognize their emotions, validate them, but also know when and how to shift away from unhelpful emotional states.

4. Social Connectivity: While resilience might seem like a personal, internal trait, it often finds its roots in the external world. Resilient individuals often have strong, supportive social networks.

These networks offer emotional support, provide different perspectives, and even present practical solutions to problems. Being deeply connected to a supportive community or having close, trusting relationships enhances an individual's capacity to navigate through adversity.

5. Growth Mindset: Coined by Carol Dweck, a "growth mindset" is the belief that abilities and intelligence can be developed through dedication and hard work. Resilient individuals, armed with this mindset, view challenges as opportunities to learn and grow. Failures are not seen as proof of inability but as a springboard for growth and stretching existing abilities.

6. Purpose and Meaning: Resilient individuals often have a clear sense of purpose in their lives. This purpose, whether tied to personal goals, relationships, or a broader cause, serves as an anchor during turbulent times.

Viktor Frankl, a Holocaust survivor and psychiatrist, emphasized the importance of finding meaning in all forms of existence, asserting that life has potential meaning under any circumstance, even the most miserable ones.

In summary, the psychology of resilient individuals is a complex interplay of mindset, emotional regulation, social connections, and intrinsic motivation.

While some might be predisposed to higher levels of resilience due to genetic or early life experiences, the consensus in psychological research is clear: resilience can be nurtured, cultivated, and strengthened through intentional effort and practice.

Benefits of Cultivating Resilience

Enhanced Coping Abilities: One of the foremost benefits of resilience is the bolstered ability to cope with challenges. In life, adversities are inevitable, ranging from daily stressors to major life-changing events. Resilient individuals tend to have a toolkit of coping strategies that they've honed over time.

These strategies enable them to navigate challenges with more ease than those who are less resilient. Rather than becoming overwhelmed by setbacks, they view them as surmountable and approach them with a problem-solving mindset. This proactive approach to life's challenges reduces the toll of stress and prevents potential mental health issues.

Emotional Regulation: Resilience contributes significantly to emotional well-being. By understanding and managing one's emotions effectively, resilient individuals prevent negative emotions like fear, anger, or sadness from spiraling out of control.

This emotional stability aids in making well-informed decisions even under pressure. Moreover, they can bounce back quicker from emotional setbacks, ensuring that they spend less time in negative emotional states and more time in positive, productive ones.

Personal Growth: Challenges and adversities, when approached with resilience, can become opportunities for personal growth. Instead of viewing setbacks as failures, resilient individuals often see them as lessons.

They dissect these experiences, extracting invaluable insights about themselves, their environment, and their relationships. This process of introspection and learning enables them to grow stronger, wiser, and more skilled, turning challenges into stepping stones for personal development.

Strengthened Relationships: Resilient individuals not only manage their own challenges but also positively influence their social circles. Their optimistic and solution-focused outlook can be infectious, uplifting those around them.

Additionally, their ability to handle conflicts and challenges means they tend to have healthier, more supportive relationships. Their empathetic understanding, born out of their own experiences with adversity, makes them compassionate friends, partners, and colleagues.

Improved Physical Health: The mental strength that comes with resilience has tangible benefits for physical health as well. Chronic stress, which can be mitigated through resilience, is known to have detrimental effects on the body, leading to conditions like hypertension, heart disease, and weakened immune function.

Resilient individuals, by effectively managing stress and emotional upheavals, protect their body from these potential harms. Their holistic health approach often also incorporates good physical habits, like regular exercise and a balanced diet, further enhancing their overall well-being.

Greater Life Satisfaction: At its core, resilience offers a richer, more fulfilling life experience. By meeting adversities head-on, with a spirit of perseverance and optimism, resilient individuals often find deeper meaning in their experiences.

They appreciate life's highs more because they've navigated its lows. This gratitude, combined with their proactive approach to challenges, results in a higher level of life satisfaction, a sense of purpose, and a zest for life that is both enviable and inspiring.

In essence, cultivating resilience is akin to building a mental and emotional muscle. Just as physical training prepares one for athletic challenges, resilience readies the mind and soul for life's myriad challenges, turning potential roadblocks into pathways for growth.

Chapter 3: Mindset Matters

In every great tale of triumph, hidden beneath layers of adversity and challenge, lies a subtle yet potent force that plays a pivotal role in the narrative of success: mindset.

It isn't just about intelligence, skills, or circumstances; it's about how one perceives and reacts to life's many challenges and opportunities. "Mindset Matters" delves deep into the psyche's terrain, exploring the paradigms that shape our reactions, choices, and ultimately, our destinies.

The ancient Greek philosopher Epictetus once proclaimed, "It's not what happens to you, but how you react to it that matters." Fast forward to today, and this timeless wisdom is backed by a plethora of modern psychological studies suggesting that the lens through which we view the world has a profound influence on our outcomes.

From the classrooms of educational institutions to the high-pressure environments of global corporations, the concept of mindset has proven to be a consistent predictor of one's ability to thrive, adapt, and overcome.

In this chapter, we will journey through the intricacies of the fixed and growth mindsets, unearthing the foundational beliefs that drive them. By understanding the importance of perspective and the role it plays in facing challenges, readers will be equipped with the knowledge to reframe their thoughts, empowering them to approach obstacles with newfound confidence and vigor.

Because when it comes to overcoming obstacles, it's not just about the size of the challenge, but the state of the mind that confronts it.

Fixed vs. Growth Mindset

Fixed Mindset:

When individuals have a fixed mindset, they believe that their qualities, talents, and abilities are fixed traits. In other words, they believe they have a certain amount of intelligence or talent, and that's that.

They see challenges as threats to their abilities, often leading them to avoid situations where they might fail or struggle. This mindset can inhibit growth because it discourages effort and persistence in the face of difficulty.

For example, a person with a fixed mindset might think, "I'm just not good at math," and as a result, they might avoid taking on challenging mathematical problems or tasks.

They often feel the need to prove themselves over and over, and they might be highly sensitive to criticism or perceived slights. Mistakes or failures become sources of distress because they view them as a reflection of their inherent capabilities.

Growth Mindset:

On the other hand, individuals with a growth mindset believe that their abilities can be developed with dedication, effort, and the right strategies. They understand that they can get smarter or more skilled in a particular area if they put in the necessary time and energy.

Challenges are viewed not as threats, but as opportunities to grow and learn. When faced with setbacks, they're more likely to persevere, believing that they can improve and overcome with the right approach.

A person with a growth mindset might think, "I might not understand this math problem now, but with some help and study, I can get it." This mindset fosters resilience, a love of learning, and a willingness to embrace challenges.

People with a growth mindset see effort as a pathway to mastery. They understand that mistakes and failures are part and parcel of the learning process and are valuable feedback for improvement.

In real-world applications, the growth mindset can be transformative. It can impact various areas of life, from education and sports to business and personal relationships.

Encouraging a growth mindset in individuals, especially from a young age, can lead to higher levels of achievement and satisfaction. It's worth noting, however, that mindsets are not absolutes.

People might exhibit a growth mindset in one area of their life (like believing they can become a better reader) and a fixed mindset in another (like thinking they can never be good at sports).

The beauty of this concept is that with awareness and effort, one can work towards cultivating a more growth-oriented mindset in all areas of life.

The Role of Perspective in Facing Challenges

At the heart of human experience lies the profound power of perspective. It shapes our understanding, governs our reactions, and carves the path for our actions. When faced with challenges, our perspective can be the determining factor between surrender and perseverance.

It's the lens through which we view our circumstances, and that lens can magnify the difficulty of our situations or focus on the potential solutions and growth opportunities they offer.

Historically, numerous luminaries and successful figures have echoed the sentiment that challenges, no matter how insurmountable they seem, are often more about perception than reality.

Consider the tale of David and Goliath. In the face of a seemingly unbeatable foe, David's perspective wasn't fixed on the giant's size and might. Instead, he saw an opponent with weaknesses that could be exploited. In modern contexts, entrepreneurs often view market challenges not as barriers but as gaps waiting to be filled with innovation.

There's a psychological dimension to this as well. Cognitive psychologists' term this as "cognitive reframing," a mental tool where individuals change the way they view a situation or challenge.

For instance, viewing a failed project not as a testament to personal incompetence but as a learning experience filled with valuable lessons. Such reframing doesn't diminish the challenge's reality but provides a constructive viewpoint, enabling individuals to tackle it with a problem-solving approach.

Moreover, perspective influences emotional responses. Two people might face the exact same setback, one might feel devastated, seeing it as a sign of their perpetual misfortune, while the other might feel motivated, considering it a nudge to change tactics or evolve.

These emotional responses are deeply intertwined with one's perspective, and they significantly influence one's resilience and determination in the face of adversity.

In essence, perspective acts as an internal compass. In the vast, tumultuous sea of challenges, it helps individuals set their direction, either guiding them towards new horizons of growth and discovery or making them circle aimlessly, fixated on the stormy waters.

By cultivating a balanced, positive, and adaptable perspective, individuals can navigate challenges with a clear vision, anchored not by the weight of their problems but buoyed by the possibilities they present.

Techniques to Shift and Reframe Mindset

1. Cognitive Behavioral Techniques:

Foundational Idea: Rooted in the principle that our thoughts shape our emotions and behaviors, cognitive behavioral techniques emphasize modifying detrimental thought patterns.

- Thought Recording: Documenting negative thoughts can help you identify and challenge them. By recognizing patterns, you can start addressing repetitive negative loops.

- Reality Testing: Question the validity of negative beliefs. Is there evidence to support them? Often, you'll find these thoughts are based on assumptions rather than facts.

- Positive Replacement: For every negative thought identified, work on substituting it with a more constructive or positive alternative.

2. Visualization Techniques:

Foundational Idea: The brain often struggles to differentiate between what is imagined and what is real. Leveraging this can help reshape mindset.

- Future Self Visualization: Regularly imagine your future successful self, experiencing the feelings and benefits of having overcome current obstacles.

- Positive Outcome Imagery: Visualize challenging situations with positive outcomes. This helps build confidence and reduces anxiety related to uncertainties.
- Guided Meditations: Using guided imagery meditations can help in visualizing positive scenarios and outcomes.

3. Affirmations and Mantras:

Foundational Idea: Repeated positive statements can rewire the brain over time and replace negative beliefs.

- Daily Affirmations: Start the day with positive affirmations related to areas you're looking to improve. Repeat them multiple times throughout the day.
- Customized Mantras: Create a personalized mantra that resonates with your goals. For instance, "I am resilient and capable of handling challenges."
- Affirmation Journals: Maintain a journal where you write down and reflect on positive affirmations regularly.

4. Growth Mindset Development:

Foundational Idea: Popularized by Carol Dweck, the growth mindset emphasizes that abilities and intelligence can be developed through dedication and hard work.

- Embrace Failures as Learning Opportunities: Instead of seeing setbacks as definitive, view them as lessons guiding your growth journey.

- Avoid Labelling: Avoid terms like "I'm not a math person" or "I can't do this." These are self-limiting beliefs.
- Celebrate Effort Over Outcome: Applaud the effort and processes, recognizing that they lead to growth and eventual success.

5. Mindfulness and Meditation:

Foundational Idea: Mindfulness practices help us stay present, thereby reducing the influence of past regrets or anxieties about the future.

- Regular Meditation: Incorporate daily meditation sessions to cultivate awareness and a non-judgmental approach to thoughts.
- Mindful Moments: Throughout the day, pause to breathe and become fully present in the moment. This practice can reduce impulsive reactions based on negative mindsets.
- Mindfulness Apps: Use applications like Headspace or Calm to guide you in practicing mindfulness effectively.

By implementing these techniques consistently, individuals can gradually shift their mindset to one that is more positive, adaptive, and resilient. Such a transformation not only aids in overcoming challenges but also in nurturing overall well-being.

Chapter 4: Lessons from Historical Figures

In every epoch of our rich tapestry of history, there have been individuals who, through their indomitable spirit, have become beacons of hope, not just for their contemporaries but for generations that followed. They are the stalwarts who faced insurmountable challenges, whether societal, personal, or both, and yet carved out legacies that still resonate today.

This chapter is not just about lauding these figures or recounting well-known tales. It's about delving deeper into their lives, understanding the adversities they faced, the choices they made, and most importantly, the resilience they showcased.

From the political arenas of South Africa and India, where Mandela and Gandhi stood against oppressive regimes, to the personal battles fought by Churchill and Lincoln, each faced a set of unique challenges.

Van Gogh and Dickinson, in their quiet corners, pursued passions in the face of obscurity, despair, and societal indifference. These individuals did not just overcome obstacles; they transformed them into stepping stones towards greatness.

As we journey through these stories, let's not just admire them from afar, but actively seek out the lessons they offer. How did they cultivate their resilience? What strategies did they employ when faced with setbacks? And how can we, in our lives, harness some of their wisdom to navigate our challenges?

Let's embark on this enlightening journey, drawing inspiration from the annals of history, to fortify our own paths forward.

Overcoming Societal Challenges

Nelson Mandela:

Nelson Mandela's life serves as an embodiment of resilience and determination in the face of oppressive societal challenges. Born in 1918 in a South Africa that was deeply entrenched in the atrocities of apartheid, Mandela grew up experiencing the brunt of racial discrimination. However, instead of succumbing to bitterness, he channeled his energies into resisting the apartheid regime.

Mandela, as a young lawyer, joined the African National Congress (ANC) and became an instrumental figure in the nonviolent protests against apartheid. However, as the regime's tactics grew more brutal, Mandela's strategies evolved, leading him to believe that armed resistance might be necessary. This commitment to his cause eventually led to his arrest and he spent 27 years in prison, enduring inhumane conditions and forced labor.

But prison couldn't break Mandela's spirit. It was during these years of confinement that Mandela's resilience truly shone, using the time to foster unity among black and white prisoners, negotiating secretly with apartheid leaders, and planning for a post-apartheid era.

Upon his release in 1990, instead of seeking revenge, Mandela sought reconciliation, working tirelessly to transition South Africa into a democracy. He eventually became the country's first Black president in 1994.

Mandela's ability to overcome societal challenges not only reshaped a nation but also set a global example of the power of perseverance, diplomacy, and forgiveness.

Mahatma Gandhi:

Mahatma Gandhi's journey as a catalyst for change began far from the shores of India, in South Africa. Facing direct racial discrimination and witnessing the broader injustice towards Indians in South Africa, Gandhi cultivated a philosophy of nonviolent resistance, or "Satyagraha."

His peaceful protests against racial pass laws in South Africa set the stage for his later work in India. Returning to India in 1915, he soon became a leader in the Indian National Congress.

India, at the time, was under British colonial rule, and the Indian populace faced economic exploitation, cultural erosion, and a lack of representation.

Gandhi, armed with his belief in nonviolent resistance, led a series of campaigns against the British. From the Non-Cooperation Movement to the Dandi March protesting the salt tax, Gandhi's peaceful yet powerful actions shook the foundations of the British Empire.

His attire, a simple hand-spun cloth, symbolized his resistance to foreign-made goods and underscored his support for Indian self-reliance.

Despite facing multiple imprisonments and personal challenges, Gandhi's indomitable spirit never wavered. His enduring commitment to nonviolence and his belief in the power of unity helped India achieve its independence in 1947.

Gandhi's approach to overcoming societal challenges was rooted in peace, unity, and an unwavering belief in the righteousness of his cause, making him not just a leader for India, but a beacon of hope and resilience for the entire world.

Both Mandela and Gandhi faced tremendous challenges, but their responses to these challenges, and their ultimate successes, have left lasting legacies that continue to inspire people worldwide.

Battling Personal Demons

Winston Churchill:

Winston Churchill, the stalwart leader who is often credited with rallying Britain to stand firm against the Nazi menace during World War II, faced his own battles beyond the political and wartime arenas. Throughout his life, Churchill grappled with what he referred to as his "black dog," a term he used to describe the bouts of depression he frequently encountered.

These episodes sometimes left him listless and fraught with a profound sense of melancholy. Yet, it's arguable that this deep introspection, fueled by his personal demons, also endowed him with the depth of character and resilience required to lead a nation under siege.

He was a man of many contrasts: a visionary leader who foresaw the dangers of Nazi Germany when many dismissed them, yet also someone who would retreat to his bed for days, overcome by depressive episodes.

In many ways, Churchill's battle with his inner demons shaped his external battles, infusing them with a sense of gravity, determination, and an unyielding spirit to endure against all odds.

Abraham Lincoln:

Abraham Lincoln, the 16th president of the United States and the leader who held the nation together during its bloodiest conflict – the Civil War, was no stranger to personal anguish. Well-documented accounts of his life suggest that Lincoln struggled with what might today be diagnosed as clinical depression.

His melancholic disposition was evident from his young adulthood, marked by introspective moods and periods of profound sadness. The weight of personal losses, including the death of his son Willie and the immense casualties of the Civil War, only deepened his sorrow.

Lincoln's contemporaries often noted his tendency to gravitate towards melancholy, but also his unparalleled ability to utilize this deep-seated sorrow as a source of strength.

Lincoln's internal struggles gave him a profound empathy and a deep understanding of human suffering, both of which became foundational in his leadership style. In the darkest hours of the nation, a leader emerged who not only understood personal suffering but also the collective agony of his country, making him uniquely positioned to guide the U.S. towards healing and unity.

Both Churchill and Lincoln are testaments to the fact that personal demons, when confronted with courage, introspection, and purpose, can be transformed into reservoirs of strength. Their leadership, molded by their individual battles, serves as an enduring testament to resilience in the face of overwhelming odds.

Pursuing Passion Against Odds

Vincent van Gogh:

Vincent van Gogh, the Dutch post-impressionist painter, is today one of the most famous and influential figures in the history of Western art. However, in his lifetime, he was neither commercially successful nor critically acclaimed. Vincent faced an array of personal challenges: mental health struggles, tumultuous relationships, and poverty, to name a few.

Despite these adversities, his passion for painting remained undeterred. He produced the entirety of his oeuvre, some 2,100 artworks, which included around 860 oil paintings, mostly in the last two years of his life. His works, characterized by bold colors, dramatic expressions, and swirling brushstrokes, were often reflections of his emotional state and his perspective on the world around him.

The external world might have seen him as a failure for the better part of his life, but Vincent's relentless commitment to his art and the intensity of his vision meant that he kept painting, even when the odds were stacked against him.

It's a poignant reminder that the measure of success isn't always immediate recognition or financial gain. Sometimes, it's the unyielding pursuit of passion against all odds, which leaves an indelible mark on history.

Emily Dickinson:

Emily Dickinson is one of America's greatest poets, known for her unique voice, unconventional style, and deeply introspective verses. But during her lifetime, she was far from the celebrated literary figure she is today.

Living a life of recluse in Amherst, Massachusetts, Emily faced societal norms that often-stifled women's voices and ambitions.

Instead of bowing to these pressures, she channeled her feelings, observations, and musings into her poetry, crafting nearly 1,800 poems.

However, only a handful of these were published during her lifetime, and those that were had been significantly edited to fit conventional norms, often to the detriment of their originality and power. Emily's passion for writing was not deterred by the lack of acknowledgment or by societal expectations.

She wrote with an authenticity and depth that transcended her era's constraints. After her death, when her complete works were eventually published in their intended form, the world came to recognize her brilliance.

Dickinson's story underscores the idea that pursuing one's passion, even in the face of obscurity and against societal expectations, can lead to posthumous recognition and an enduring legacy.

Chapter 5: Modern Titans and Their Resilience Techniques

In a rapidly changing world, the tales of persistence from yesteryears might seem distant, almost mythological. But resilience is not just a relic of the past; it's an ever-evolving trait, adapting and thriving amidst contemporary challenges.

As we navigate the whirlwind of the digital era, globalization, and unprecedented change, there are modern-day titans among us who exemplify the spirit of tenacity. These are individuals who've not only shaped industries but also redefined norms, challenged the status quo, and risen from the ashes of their failures to become icons of our era.

In this chapter, we will delve into the lives and stories of some of these influential figures. From business magnates who've reimagined industries to athletes who've pushed the boundaries of human capabilities, to artists who've dared to think differently, their stories are a testament to the fact that resilience is as relevant today as it ever was.

But more than just their successes, we aim to unearth the techniques they employed to bounce back from setbacks. What mental frameworks did they adopt? How did they handle criticism and navigate the maze of modern pressures? By decoding their strategies, we hope to offer you a roadmap, a set of actionable insights that you can integrate into your own journey of overcoming obstacles.

Prepare to be inspired, educated, and equipped to face your challenges with renewed vigor, as we uncover the resilience techniques of the world's most successful modern titans.

Business Magnates

Elon Musk:

Elon Musk, a visionary entrepreneur and innovator, is often equated with iconic figures like Steve Jobs or Thomas Edison due to his audacious goals and accomplishments in various industries. Born in South Africa in 1971, Musk's entrepreneurial journey began early when he sold a homemade video game at the age of 12.

Later, moving to the United States, his first major success came with Zip2, a software company he co-founded, which was eventually sold for nearly $300 million. He then co-founded X.com, an online payment company that after a series of evolutions became the global entity known as PayPal.

However, Elon's ambitions were far from satiated with these ventures. He invested his own money to start SpaceX with a vision to make space travel affordable and eventually colonize Mars. Similarly, with Tesla, Inc., he revolutionized the automotive industry by bringing electric cars to the forefront, challenging traditional automotive giants.

But Musk didn't stop at cars and rockets; with endeavors like Neuralink, he's delving into brain-computer interfaces, and with The Boring Company, he's exploring ways to reduce traffic congestion via underground transportation.

While his methods are sometimes seen as unconventional and his timelines overly optimistic, there's no denying the profound impact Elon Musk has had on the aerospace, automotive, and energy sectors.

Oprah Winfrey:

Oprah Winfrey, a name synonymous with inspiration and empowerment, has a rags-to-riches story that personifies the American Dream. Born into poverty in rural Mississippi in 1954, Oprah faced numerous hardships in her early life, including abuse and teenage pregnancy.

However, she turned her life around with sheer determination, landing a job in radio while still in high school, which eventually led to her discovering her passion for media and broadcasting. Her major break came in 1983 when she took over the hosting duties for a low-rated local Chicago talk show.

The show was revamped and renamed "The Oprah Winfrey Show", and its unique blend of confessional storytelling and uplifting interviews quickly propelled it to the top of the ratings.

Oprah's empathetic style, combined with her business acumen, led to her becoming the wealthiest African American of the 20th century. But her influence extends far beyond TV. She's an Academy Award-nominated actress, a producer, and a philanthropist. Oprah's Book Club turned unknown authors into best-sellers overnight. Moreover, her philanthropic efforts have been monumental, especially in the areas of education and disaster relief.

Her establishment of the Oprah Winfrey Leadership Academy for Girls in South Africa is a testament to her commitment to empowering the next generation. In business, media, and philanthropy, Oprah Winfrey is a figure of unparalleled influence and impact.

Sports Figures

Serena Williams:

Serena Williams, born in Saginaw, Michigan, in 1981, is often regarded as one of the greatest tennis players of all time. Her journey to the pinnacle of tennis, however, was replete with challenges that required immense resilience.

Born to a family with limited means, Williams and her sister, Venus, started their training on the cracked courts of Compton, California.

The Williams sisters faced skepticism from traditional tennis circles due to their unorthodox training methods, as they were coached by their father, Richard Williams, who had no formal experience in tennis.

Beyond the challenges in her formative years, Serena's resilience shone bright as she faced severe health issues, including life-threatening pulmonary embolisms following the birth of her daughter in 2017. Despite these challenges, her determination remained unshaken.

With 23 Grand Slam titles to her name, Serena's career is a testament to her indomitable spirit, proving that with talent, hard work, and resilience, one can overcome even the most formidable of obstacles.

Off the court, she's been a staunch advocate for women's rights, especially for equal pay in sports, further showcasing her grit and determination to challenge the status quo.

Michael Jordan:

Michael Jordan, often celebrated as the greatest basketball player ever, was born in Brooklyn, New York, in 1963. His success story is synonymous with the power of perseverance. As a young athlete, Jordan faced early setbacks, the most notable being cut from his high school varsity basketball team during his sophomore year.

Instead of capitulating to this disappointment, he used it as fuel to work even harder. This setback and his response to it became foundational to Jordan's approach to adversity.

Throughout his illustrious NBA career with the Chicago Bulls and briefly with the Washington Wizards, Jordan faced numerous on-court challenges.

He faced teams that were built specifically to counter his style of play, endured physical games that tested his limits, and dealt with the immense pressure of being in the global spotlight.

Despite these hurdles, he secured six NBA championships and earned five MVP awards. Jordan's resilience wasn't limited to his sporting career. After a brief retirement from basketball, he pursued baseball, a testament to his versatile athletic prowess and desire to continuously challenge himself.

While his baseball stint was short-lived and less acclaimed, it demonstrated his commitment to reinvention.

Beyond sports, Jordan experienced personal tragedies, including the loss of his father in 1993, which deeply affected him.

Yet, in each phase of his life, whether facing professional setbacks or personal losses, Jordan's resilience and commitment to excellence shone through, making him a beacon of inspiration for many around the globe.

Both Williams and Jordan are not just exemplary athletes but also embodiments of the power of perseverance and resilience in the face of adversity. Their careers offer invaluable lessons on the importance of hard work, self-belief, and an unyielding spirit.

Entertainment Leaders

Steven Spielberg:

Steven Spielberg, one of the most celebrated directors and producers in the history of cinema, has contributed a collection of iconic films spanning various genres. Born in 1946 in Cincinnati, Ohio, Spielberg's passion for filmmaking began in his early years.

However, his journey to the zenith of Hollywood wasn't without challenges. Spielberg was rejected multiple times from the University of Southern California's School of Cinematic Arts, a turn of events that could have dissuaded many. Yet, he persisted, making short films and networking relentlessly.

His breakthrough came with the thriller "Duel" in 1971, which led to a string of successes including "Jaws," "E.T. the Extra-Terrestrial," "Indiana Jones," and "Schindler's List." Spielberg's tenacity, combined with his innate ability to tell stories that resonate universally, transformed the face of cinema.

Overcoming personal and professional hurdles, from dyslexia to industry skepticism, Spielberg's resilience and vision solidified his position as a vanguard of the entertainment world.

J.K. Rowling:

Joanne Rowling, known worldwide as J.K. Rowling, is the mastermind behind the globally adored "Harry Potter" series. Born in Yate, England, in 1965, Rowling's journey to becoming one of the world's best-selling authors is a tale of resilience in its own right.

The idea for Harry Potter came to her during a train journey, and she began crafting the magical world, characters, and plots. However, life threw her several curveballs.

From the loss of her mother, to a divorce, to facing financial constraints while raising her daughter as a single mother, Rowling experienced numerous hardships.

During these testing times, she penned the first Harry Potter book, which was subsequently rejected by a slew of publishers. Yet, her perseverance bore fruit when Bloomsbury Publishing gave "Harry Potter and the Philosopher's Stone" a chance, a decision that led to a literary and cinematic phenomenon.

J.K. Rowling's narrative abilities combined with her personal journey of overcoming obstacles make her not just a prominent entertainment figure but also a beacon of hope for aspiring writers and dreamers worldwide.

Both these figures exemplify the spirit of determination and resilience, overcoming numerous challenges to leave indelible marks on the entertainment industry.

Chapter 6: The Role of Failure in Building Resilience

In our ceaseless pursuit of success, we often view failure as the formidable enemy, a dark cloud casting shadows on our ambitions and dreams. Society's glorification of achievement, fueled further by the glossy realms of social media, has fashioned an illusion where setbacks are concealed and only triumphs are showcased.

But what if we've been interpreting this all wrong? What if failure, rather than being the antagonist of our story, is actually the unsung hero?

This chapter delves deep into the intricate relationship between failure and resilience. It peels back the layers of our preconceived notions, inviting readers to see failure not as the end but as a crucial milestone on the journey to success.

Every stumble, every missed step, and every setback can be a stepping stone, propelling us forward with renewed vigor, fortified strength, and invaluable lessons.

Through illuminating tales of well-known figures who embraced their failures and the lesser-known stories of everyday heroes among us, we will discover the transformative power of mistakes and mishaps.

Join us as we redefine failure, understanding its quintessential role in molding, shaping, and, most importantly, fortifying our resilience. Let's unravel the truth that behind every great success often lies a series of failures, and it is our response to these failures that determines our true trajectory.

Why Failure Is A Stepping Stone to Success

The Inherent Nature of Progress: At its core, progress in any domain is inherently a trial-and-error process. From inventors and scientists to artists and entrepreneurs, numerous attempts often precede breakthroughs. Thomas Edison, for instance, made thousands of unsuccessful attempts before finally inventing the light bulb.

He famously remarked, "I have not failed. I've just found 10,000 ways that won't work." This perspective views failure not as a dead end, but as a learning opportunity, a natural part of the process toward achieving a goal.

Learning Through Mistakes: Failures, mistakes, and setbacks often provide the most potent lessons. When everything goes smoothly, it's easy to move forward without deep reflection or understanding. However, failure forces individuals to confront what went wrong.

This confrontation often leads to insights about necessary changes, adjustments, or improvements. As a result, individuals and organizations can iterate and evolve, turning setbacks into setups for future success.

Building Resilience and Character: Encountering failure and bouncing back from it builds resilience, a crucial trait for long-term success. This resilience ensures that when faced with future challenges, individuals have the mental and emotional fortitude to endure, adapt, and overcome.

Moreover, enduring failures and persisting in the face of adversity often cultivates character, instilling values such as patience, perseverance, and humility.

Validating and Refining Ideas: Especially in the realms of business and innovation, not all ideas are destined for success. Some are before their time, while others may not be viable due to market conditions, technical limitations, or other factors.

Failure serves as a filter, helping entrepreneurs and innovators validate or refine their ideas. By identifying what doesn't work, they can focus on optimizing what might work, leading them closer to successful solutions.

Developing a Growth Mindset: Dr. Carol Dweck, a psychologist and researcher, introduced the concept of the "growth mindset", the belief that abilities and intelligence can be developed with effort, training, and perseverance.

People with a growth mindset see failure not as evidence of unintelligence or incapability, but as a valuable source of growth, an opportunity to evolve. Embracing failure is foundational to fostering this mindset, which is often linked to greater achievements and success.

Broadening Perspectives and Encouraging Innovation: Sometimes, when our initial efforts fail, they push us out of our comfort zones and traditional ways of thinking. This shift can lead to innovative solutions we might not have considered otherwise. In this way, failure can be a catalyst for creativity, urging us to approach problems from different angles or to explore new methodologies.

In essence, while failure can be disheartening in the short term, its long-term value is immeasurable. It serves as a teacher, a motivator, a refiner of ideas, and, paradoxically, one of the most reliable pathways to success. The key lies in not avoiding failure, but in embracing it, learning from it, and using it as a springboard for future endeavors.

Famous Failures and Their Subsequent Successes

Albert Einstein:

Often considered one of the most brilliant minds in history, Albert Einstein wasn't always seen as such. During his early years, he struggled with speech, leading some to believe he had a learning disability.

Moreover, he didn't speak until the age of four and didn't read until seven. His teachers often thought he was lazy, and he even failed the entrance exam to the Swiss Federal Institute of Technology.

However, Einstein's later years debunked all these early misconceptions. He developed the theory of relativity, one of the two pillars of modern physics, and was awarded the Nobel Prize in Physics in 1921. His name is now synonymous with "genius."

Thomas Edison:

Known as one of the most prolific inventors in history, Thomas Edison's journey to success was paved with a multitude of failures. One of his most famous failures was the creation of a practical electric light bulb. He encountered thousands of unsuccessful attempts before he finally achieved a functional design.

When asked about his failures, he once remarked, "I have not failed. I've just found 10,000 ways that won't work." Edison's resilience resulted in the patenting of over 1,000 inventions, including the phonograph, the motion picture camera, and improvements to the electric power grid.

J.K. Rowling:

The creator of the 'Harry Potter' series, J.K. Rowling's early life was marked by significant personal and professional challenges. After a short-lived marriage, she found herself a single mother living on welfare. Her first Harry Potter manuscript was rejected by multiple publishing houses.

However, when Bloomsbury Publishing finally took a chance on it, the world was introduced to the magical realm of Hogwarts.

The series has since become one of the best-selling book series in history, and Rowling's life story serves as a testament to the importance of perseverance and believing in one's vision.

Walt Disney:

Today, the name 'Disney' is synonymous with animated films, theme parks, and a media empire. However, Walt Disney's initial forays into the business world were far from successful. His first animation company went bankrupt. He was fired from a newspaper for "lacking imagination and having no original ideas."

Despite these setbacks, Disney never gave up. He moved to Hollywood and began the Disney Brothers Studio. From there, he introduced the world to Mickey Mouse, and the rest, as they say, is history.

His legacy includes the creation of Disneyland and Walt Disney World, and he became a household name worldwide.

Oprah Winfrey:

Before becoming a media mogul and billionaire, Oprah Winfrey faced numerous personal and professional setbacks. She grew up in poverty, faced abuse during her childhood, and was fired from her job as a television reporter because she was "unfit for TV."

Undeterred, Oprah continued to pursue her passion for media. She transformed a low-rated local Chicago talk show into "The Oprah Winfrey Show," which went on to become the highest-rated talk show in history. Beyond television, her influence expanded to magazines, radio, acting, and philanthropy.

These examples underscore the age-old adage: "Failure is not the opposite of success; it's a part of success." Each of these iconic figures faced significant obstacles but viewed them as learning experiences rather than dead-ends. Their stories inspire millions and illuminate the potential within each of us to rise above setbacks and achieve greatness.

Embracing and Learning from Failure

Failure, often perceived with dread and aversion, is an inescapable part of the human journey. However, the most transformative experiences often arise from these stumbling blocks.

Embracing failure means accepting it not as the end but as an integral part of one's growth trajectory. This embrace isn't about celebrating setbacks, but about viewing them as opportunities to glean insights, correct course, and refine approaches.

Historically, countless innovations and success stories have had failure as a precursor. Take, for instance, Thomas Edison.

When asked about his 10,000 unsuccessful attempts to invent the light bulb, he remarked, "I haven't failed. I've just found 10,000 ways that won't work." This statement encapsulates the essence of viewing failures as mere stepping stones.

When we dissect failure, we often find it's not a void but a repository of valuable lessons, waiting to be unraveled.

Learning from failure is the next crucial step after embracing it. This requires introspection, feedback analysis, and a determination to act upon the acquired knowledge.

When one encounters a setback, it's imperative to ask: "Why did this happen? What could I have done differently? What can I do to ensure this doesn't recur?" Such inquiries foster growth and shield one from repeating the same mistakes.

Moreover, sharing and discussing failures with mentors, peers, or teams can offer fresh perspectives and unforeseen solutions.

In today's rapidly evolving world, where innovation is celebrated, the risk of failure is high. Companies like Google have embedded the idea of 'failing fast' in their work culture, understanding that quick failures lead to quicker improvements and innovations.

The tech industry's iterative design processes, for instance, are based on the principle of learning from small failures to avoid larger ones in the future.

In essence, while society often glorifies success and shuns failure, it's the latter that shapes character, imparts wisdom, and paves the way for lasting achievement.

Embracing and learning from failure is not just a skill but a mindset, one that acknowledges the imperfections of the human experience but is relentless in its pursuit of growth and excellence.

Chapter 7: Strategies to Cultivate Resilience

In the tapestry of life, we often find the threads of challenges and obstacles intricately woven alongside those of success and joy. While the narratives of history's great figures and today's luminaries give testimony to the power of resilience, one might wonder:

Is resilience an innate trait, or can it be cultivated? The good news is that resilience, like a muscle, can be strengthened and developed with time and practice.

In this chapter, we will delve deep into the heart of resilience, breaking down its components and revealing actionable strategies that can fortify this crucial aspect of our psyche.

Whether you're facing a personal setback, a professional challenge, or simply preparing for the unpredictable journey of life, these strategies offer a roadmap to not just bounce back, but to rise higher with each hurdle.

Embarking on this journey, we will uncover practices from various cultures, insights from psychology, and time-tested techniques that have helped individuals traverse their darkest hours. Let's begin this transformative voyage to discover the wellspring of strength that lies within each of us.

Mental Conditioning and Exercises

Mental Conditioning:

Mental conditioning refers to the training of one's mind to improve performance, reaction to stress, or specific outcomes in various situations. Much like how an athlete conditions their body for peak physical performance, mental conditioning focuses on honing the mind's capabilities.

This practice often revolves around refining thought patterns, beliefs, and emotional responses. Mental conditioning isn't about eliminating negative thoughts but rather learning to recognize and redirect them. It's about cultivating a proactive mindset that helps individuals anticipate, prepare for, and navigate challenges.

Successful individuals from all walks of life, from athletes to CEOs, often incorporate mental conditioning into their routines, recognizing that a strong, resilient mind can significantly affect one's success.

Some key aspects of mental conditioning include visualization, positive reinforcement, setting clear intentions, and managing stress and anxiety.

Mental Conditioning Exercises:

Visualization: This involves vividly imagining a scenario or outcome you want to achieve. Athletes, for instance, often visualize their moves, actions, and the desired result (like scoring a goal) before they even set foot in the game.

Visualization reinforces neural pathways, helping the brain align with one's goals and intentions. It's not merely about daydreaming but actively feeling and experiencing the envisioned success.

Affirmations: Positive affirmations help in rewiring the brain's thought patterns. By repeatedly affirming a positive belief or statement, individuals can gradually diminish self-doubt and enhance self-confidence. An example would be reciting, "I am capable of handling challenges" or "I am deserving of success and happiness."

Mindfulness and Meditation: Grounding exercises help individuals remain present, reducing anxiety and overthinking. Techniques such as focused breathing, body scans, or guided meditations allow for a clearer mind, better concentration, and reduced stress. They also improve self-awareness, enabling individuals to recognize and manage negative thought patterns swiftly.

Cognitive Behavioral Therapy Techniques (CBT): CBT exercises can be used to identify and challenge negative beliefs or distortions. For instance, if someone thinks, "I always mess things up," they can challenge this belief by listing times they've succeeded or noting that everyone makes mistakes, and it doesn't define their entire character.

Stress Reduction Techniques: Techniques such as progressive muscle relaxation, where individuals tense and then relax different muscle groups, can help reduce physical manifestations of stress.

Similarly, the "5-4-3-2-1" grounding exercise, where one identifies five things they can see, four they can touch, three they can hear, two they can smell, and one they can taste, can divert attention from stressors and anchor the individual in the present.

Journaling: Writing down thoughts, feelings, and reflections can provide clarity, allow for emotional release, and help in problem-solving. It's a way to converse with oneself, to understand patterns, and to set intentions.

Incorporating these exercises into a daily or weekly routine can greatly improve mental agility, resilience, and overall well-being. Over time, as with any form of training, consistency in mental conditioning can lead to notable positive changes in one's mindset and reactions to challenges.

The Importance of Self-Care and Its Role

The Importance of Self-Care:

In today's fast-paced world, the challenges of daily life can easily become overwhelming. From the constant barrage of work responsibilities to the demands of family life, from the incessant buzz of social media notifications to the personal aspirations that never seem to get our full attention, we are perpetually pulled in a myriad of directions.

Amidst this whirlwind of obligations and distractions, the significance of self-care often gets overshadowed. Yet, self-care is not a luxury, it's a necessity. It is the foundation upon which our mental, emotional, and physical well-being rests.

Self-care refers to the deliberate actions we take to care for our health and happiness. These actions range from simple habits like getting adequate sleep and maintaining a balanced diet to more profound practices like meditation, journaling, and seeking therapeutic support.

By prioritizing self-care, individuals can recharge their batteries, reduce the impact of stress, and cultivate a sense of inner peace. The adage "You can't pour from an empty cup" rings especially true here. By not taking care of ourselves, we risk burnout, increased susceptibility to illness, and an overall decline in well-being.

The Role of Self-Care:

Physical Health: Regular self-care practices, like exercising, eating nutritious foods, and getting enough rest, play a pivotal role in maintaining physical health.

They help improve immunity, reduce the risk of chronic diseases, and increase longevity. When we feel physically robust and energetic, we're better equipped to tackle daily challenges.

Mental and Emotional Well-being: Self-care is intricately linked with mental health. Activities such as meditation, journaling, or simply taking a break from digital devices can significantly reduce anxiety, depression, and feelings of overwhelm.

By dedicating time to self-reflection and understanding our emotions, we foster resilience and a stronger emotional equilibrium.

Enhanced Productivity: Contrary to the notion that constant work leads to greater output, regular breaks and self-care practices can boost productivity. They provide the mind a necessary respite, leading to increased focus, creativity, and efficiency upon return.

Improved Relationships: When we're well-rested and mentally at peace, we're better communicators and more empathetic listeners.

Self-care allows us to approach relationships from a place of understanding and compassion, rather than stress and reactivity. It enhances our ability to connect with others and nurture meaningful bonds.

Personal Growth: Prioritizing self-care can lead to profound insights about one's desires, goals, and life's purpose. By spending time with oneself, free from external influences, one can tap into inner wisdom, leading to growth and self-actualization.

In essence, self-care is far from being a selfish act. It's a commitment to oneself, a promise to honor one's well-being amidst the cacophony of life.

By recognizing its importance and actively integrating it into daily routines, individuals not only uplift their own lives but also positively impact their communities, paving the way for holistic well-being and contentment.

Developing a Support System: Mentors, Peers, and Family

Mentors:

In the journey of personal and professional growth, mentors play an instrumental role. These are individuals who have walked the path before us, acquired wisdom through experience, and can offer guidance, insights, and advice when we face challenges.

Having a mentor is like having a personalized roadmap; they can help us navigate obstacles, foresee potential pitfalls, and encourage us to take routes we might not have considered.

Beyond professional guidance, mentors can offer life lessons that textbooks and courses cannot. The bond between a mentor and mentee transcends a mere transactional relationship.

It's often forged in trust, respect, and mutual learning. To cultivate a mentoring relationship, one must be proactive, seeking out those whose work and journey align with their aspirations, reaching out for guidance, and committing to the growth process.

Peers:

Peers act as our contemporaries on this journey, and their importance cannot be overstated. These are the individuals who are walking alongside us, experiencing similar challenges, aspirations, and milestones. Sharing experiences with peers can offer a sense of camaraderie and understanding that's unique.

They can provide feedback from a perspective that's closely aligned with our own, given their shared context. Group brainstorming, mutual motivation, and friendly competition with peers can lead to accelerated growth and learning.

Moreover, peers can act as a mirror, reflecting our strengths, areas for improvement, and sometimes, showing us facets of ourselves we weren't aware of.

Building a strong peer network involves active participation in community events, workshops, online forums, and being open to collaborations.

Family:

Family acts as the bedrock of support for most individuals. They provide emotional, psychological, and often, practical support in our pursuits. Families are our first cheerleaders, our safe space to retreat when things get tough, and our confidants when we're in doubt.

Their role in developing resilience cannot be understated. Even though family members might not always understand the intricacies of our professional or personal challenges, their unwavering faith and love offer a cushioning against the harshness of failures and setbacks.

Keeping open communication with family, involving them in our journey, and valuing their perspective can further enhance the support they provide.

While it's natural to seek independence and carve out our path, it's essential to recognize the foundational role family plays in our overall well-being and resilience.

In essence, while each of these support pillars, mentors, peers, and family, offers a distinct form of guidance and encouragement, in tandem, they create a robust system.

This system can bolster us against adversities, provide diverse insights, and enrich our journey with shared experiences and unconditional love.

Chapter 8: Tools for Overcoming Obstacles

Welcome to Chapter 8, where we delve into the nitty-gritty of overcoming life's numerous challenges: the tools and resources you can use to navigate your way around, over, or through the obstacles you face. It's one thing to understand the mindset behind resilience and the psychological strategies that foster it, as we've explored in previous chapters. Still, it's another to have a tangible set of tools at your fingertips, ready to be employed when adversity strikes.

In this chapter, we focus on offering you a "toolkit" filled with practical, actionable items that you can implement right away. Think of this chapter as the utility belt of your resilience armor, the swiss army knife in your challenge-conquering arsenal. Whether you're up against personal issues like stress and emotional upheaval or external hurdles like professional setbacks and societal barriers, there's a tool in this chapter designed to help you manage and overcome it.

We'll examine traditional tools like meditation and mindfulness exercises that have stood the test of time, benefiting millions in their quest for a resilient life. We'll also delve into modern resources like technology and apps specifically designed to help build resilience and overcome obstacles.

Because we all face a unique set of challenges, no single tool will be universally effective. Instead, we offer a range of options so you can custom-tailor your approach to overcoming obstacles, enabling you to select the techniques that resonate most closely with your personal journey.

Role of Meditation in Personal Growth

Meditation, an age-old practice rooted in various cultures and traditions around the world, has gained significant recognition in modern times for its profound impact on personal growth and well-being.

At its core, meditation involves focusing one's mind and eliminating the influx of thoughts, leading to enhanced awareness and attention. Through consistent practice, meditation facilitates a deeper connection with one's inner self, fostering clarity, peace, and harmony.

One of the most transformative aspects of meditation is its ability to manage and reduce stress. In a world rife with external pressures and constant stimuli, the mind often struggles to find reprieve.

Meditation offers this sanctuary, a space where the mind can relax, rejuvenate, and regain its equilibrium. Neuroscientific research has illuminated how meditation can reduce the production of cortisol, the body's primary stress hormone, thus playing a pivotal role in managing anxiety and related disorders.

Furthermore, meditation paves the way for improved concentration and focus. In an age of distractions, maintaining undivided attention on tasks becomes challenging. Regular meditation practices have shown to enhance the brain's ability to concentrate, making individuals more productive and efficient in their personal and professional lives.

Mindfulness and its Transformative Power

Mindfulness, a form of meditation in itself, emphasizes living in the present moment with full awareness, without judgment. Instead of getting lost in the past's regrets or the future's anxieties, mindfulness anchors individuals firmly in the 'now,' allowing them to experience life more fully and authentically.

The act of being mindful enables individuals to cultivate a heightened awareness of their thoughts, feelings, bodily sensations, and the surrounding environment. This heightened awareness is not just passive observation. It's an active engagement that allows individuals to recognize and accept their experiences, both positive and negative, without getting overly reactive or overwhelmed by them.

One of the most significant benefits of mindfulness is emotional regulation. By observing one's thoughts and emotions without attachment, individuals can gain perspective, seeing their feelings as transient states rather than defining truths. This detachment allows for better control over reactions, leading to more thoughtful responses to challenging situations rather than impulsive reactions.

Additionally, mindfulness plays a crucial role in enhancing self-awareness. By regularly checking in with oneself and recognizing patterns of thought and behavior, individuals can identify areas of personal growth and make conscious choices to evolve and transform.

Both meditation and mindfulness, though interrelated, offer unique tools and perspectives that assist in personal growth. Their cumulative effect is a more cantered, aware, and balanced individual capable of navigating life's challenges with grace and poise.

Practical Tools: Journaling, Vision Boards, Affirmations

1. Journaling:

Journaling is a timeless and deeply introspective tool that has aided countless individuals in navigating their innermost feelings, thoughts, and reactions. At its core, journaling offers a private, judgment-free space for self-expression, allowing a person to clarify their thoughts, acknowledge emotions, and track their personal growth over time.

When facing challenges, it acts as a reflection medium, providing a space to dissect the issue, vent frustrations, and brainstorm solutions. The consistent act of writing can lead to enhanced problem-solving skills, as it forces the mind to approach issues from various angles.

Moreover, looking back on previous entries can serve as a powerful reminder of past obstacles overcome, reinforcing one's belief in their resilience and capabilities. The beauty of journaling lies in its flexibility; whether one opts for structured prompts or free-flowing prose, the act of putting pen to paper can be profoundly therapeutic and enlightening.

Dive Deeper into Self-Discovery with Our Latest Release!

Do you ever find yourself seeking clarity about who you truly are? Yearning to uncover deeper truths hidden beneath the surface of daily life? Our newest journal is crafted just for you!

Introducing:

The Introspection Journal: 365 Prompts to Understand Yourself

Why this journal is a MUST-HAVE:

Personal Growth: Unlock insights about your beliefs, dreams, emotions, and more.

Daily Reflection: A structured, year-long journey through thought-provoking prompts.

Enhanced Self-Awareness: Discover patterns, embrace growth, and achieve greater clarity in your life decisions.

Whether you're a seasoned journaler or just beginning your journey, this journal promises a transformative experience. Each prompt is designed to guide you deeper into your mind, heart, and soul. Embrace the opportunity to become your own best friend, confidant, and guide.

Embark on a journey of introspection and self-love. Claim your journal today and embrace the beauty of true self-awareness!

Get it now at InspirationDB.com/Journal

2. Vision Boards:

A vision board is a tangible representation of one's aspirations, dreams, and goals. By collecting images, quotes, and other visual elements that resonate with a person's desires, they create a powerful visual stimulus that keeps their objectives front and canter.

When faced with obstacles, a glance at a vision board serves as a vivid reminder of the 'why' behind their journey, rekindling motivation and focus.

Beyond motivation, vision boards are also tools for manifestation. The consistent visual reinforcement can, over time, shape one's mindset, actions, and habits, subtly aligning them with their goals.

Creating a vision board is both a proactive and reactive tool: proactive in setting clear intentions for the future, and reactive in serving as a beacon during challenging times, guiding the way back to one's path.

3. Affirmations:

Affirmations are positive, empowering statements that, when repeated, aim to overwrite limiting beliefs and negative thought patterns.

Rooted in the realms of cognitive behavioral therapy and neurolinguistic programming, affirmations work on the principle that our beliefs shape our actions, and consequently, our reality.

By actively choosing to feed the mind empowering statements, individuals can cultivate a more positive, resilient mindset.

Especially during times of adversity, repeating affirmations like "I am capable of overcoming any challenge" or "Every obstacle presents an opportunity to grow" can provide the mental strength to push through.

For affirmations to be effective, they should be phrased in the present tense, be positive in nature, and resonate genuinely with the individual. Over time, with consistency, these positive statements can shift one's internal narrative, leading to more constructive actions and reactions in the face of challenges.

Each of these tools, whether used independently or in conjunction, offers a unique pathway for individuals to understand themselves better, stay focused on their goals, and foster the mental resilience necessary to overcome life's inevitable hurdles.

Technology That Can Aid Resilience Building

Digital Therapy and Counselling Platforms:

One of the primary tools that technology offers in the realm of resilience-building is access to therapy and counselling through digital platforms. Apps with AI-driven algorithms or offer remote counselling with real therapists, breaking the barriers of physical location, stigma, or cost.

These platforms allow individuals to gain insights into their mental state, develop coping mechanisms, and find support in moments of distress.

With the pandemic-induced isolation, the importance of such platforms became even more pronounced, as they bridged the gap between those seeking mental health assistance and professionals who could guide them.

Mindfulness and Meditation Apps:

Mindfulness and meditation are proven techniques to enhance resilience by teaching individuals to stay present, manage their reactions to stressors, and foster a calmer demeanor.

Apps with guided meditations, sleep stories, and breathing exercises tailored to various needs, whether it's anxiety reduction, improved focus, or better sleep. With daily practices and reminders, these tools embed resilience-building practices into users' everyday routines.

Habit-Tracking and Personal Development Tools:

Building resilience often involves the cultivation of positive habits that enhance one's capacity to manage stress and overcome challenges. Applications which allow users to set, track, and maintain habits.

By visualizing progress and maintaining streaks, these apps not only bolster the desired behavior but also cultivate a mindset of persistence and consistency, foundational to resilience.

Learning and Skill Development Platforms:

Resilience isn't just about managing distress but also about growing from challenges. Platforms which offer courses on personal development, cognitive behavior therapy, and other resilience-enhancing subjects.

By fostering a culture of lifelong learning and adaptability, they allow users to equip themselves with knowledge and skills, making them more resilient in the face of changing life circumstances or career challenges.

Social Connection and Support Group Platforms:

Resilience is often bolstered by community and connection. Technology has paved the way for various platforms where people can find like-minded individuals, support groups, or communities facing similar challenges.

Websites and apps or specialized forums allow individuals to connect over shared interests or challenges, offering mutual support and exchange of resilience-building techniques.

Biofeedback and Wearable Technology:

Wearable devices or headband offer biofeedback about one's physiological responses. They can track sleep patterns, heart rate variability, and even levels of concentration during meditation.

By making users aware of their physiological responses to stressors, these devices enable them to adopt strategies that can modulate such responses, essentially training the body and mind to react more calmly to stress.

In summary, technology serves as a potent ally in resilience-building by providing tools, platforms, and resources that were previously inaccessible or non-existent.

From mental health support to habit cultivation and community connection, the digital realm offers numerous avenues to enhance resilience, preparing individuals to better face life's challenges.

Stan Barren

Chapter 9: Staying Motivated When the Going Gets Tough

If you've ever run a marathon, hiked a mountain, or even simply cleaned out a long-neglected garage, you're familiar with "the wall", that moment when the energy drains from your limbs, your enthusiasm wanes, and you wonder why you ever started this task in the first place.

This chapter is about that crucial phase in overcoming obstacles: the part where the initial burst of energy has dissipated, and you find yourself questioning your ability to continue. It's the proverbial 20th mile of the marathon, the steep climb just before the summit, or the last set of weights in your exercise routine.

When tackling obstacles, especially significant ones that require prolonged effort, maintaining your momentum is often harder than getting started. The honeymoon phase wears off, reality sets in, and what was once an exciting challenge becomes a grinding chore.

But it is precisely during these moments that resilience comes into play the most. The truly successful people, the ones whose stories we've examined in the earlier chapters, don't just have the courage to start; they also possess the tenacity to finish.

In this chapter, we'll delve into the concept of sustaining motivation when the going gets tough. We'll discuss the psychological underpinnings of motivation, explore how a sense of purpose can be your guiding light during dark times, and investigate techniques to rekindle passion and drive when they start to flicker.

Along the way, we'll hear inspirational anecdotes from high achievers across different domains, those who've managed to push through their own versions of "the wall" to attain their goals.

So, if you've ever found yourself at that pivotal moment where giving up seems more attractive than going on, read ahead. The tools and insights in this chapter might just give you the fuel you need to break through your own barriers and keep moving towards success.

The Importance of Purpose And 'Why'

The Importance of Purpose

At the core of human existence lies an innate desire to have meaning, direction, and a sense of belonging. This is where the concept of 'purpose' plays a pivotal role. Having a purpose goes beyond just daily routines or achieving short-term goals.

It is the driving force that fuels passion, determination, and the will to persevere. Purpose provides a sense of clarity amidst chaos, guiding individuals through the challenges and uncertainties of life.

It's like the North Star; while it may not dictate every decision, it provides a consistent direction to move towards. Studies have even shown that people with a clear sense of purpose tend to live longer, have better cardiovascular health, and even lower levels of neuroticism.

From an evolutionary perspective, those with a clear purpose are more focused, driven, and adaptive, making them more likely to overcome challenges and hence, thrive.

Introducing "The Ultimate Guide to Finding Your Life's Purpose."

Whether you're at a crossroads, feeling lost, or simply curious about what makes life truly meaningful, this comprehensive e-book has the insights, exercises, and stories to illuminate your path.

And here's the best part: We're giving it away for FREE! Don't miss out! Subscribe to our email newsletter now and get instant access to "The Ultimate Guide to Finding Your Life's Purpose." Discover the passion, meaning, and drive that's waiting within you.

Get now from InspirationDB.com/FREE

The Power of 'Why'

While 'purpose' provides the broader direction, understanding one's 'why' is the catalyst that ignites action. Simon Sinek, a motivational speaker and author, famously emphasized that people don't buy 'what' you do; they buy 'why' you do it.

The 'why' is the underlying reason, the deep-seated motivation behind actions and decisions. It's the intrinsic motivator when external motivations wane. For example, two individuals might be working late hours on a project.

One does it because they fear reprimand from a supervisor; the other does it because they believe in the project's potential to bring about positive change. While both might complete the task, the latter is driven by a deeper 'why,' making their dedication, passion, and even the quality of work fundamentally different.

When faced with obstacles, understanding one's 'why' can reignite the passion and determination to push through. It serves as a reminder of the bigger picture and the reason one embarked on a particular journey in the first place.

In essence, both purpose and 'why' are deeply intertwined, serving as the compass and fuel, respectively, for the journey of life. When combined, they become an unstoppable force, guiding individuals toward meaningful, passionate, and dedicated lives.

Techniques to Reignite Passion and Drive

1. Self-Reflection and Reconnection:

At the core of dwindling passion often lies a disconnect from one's initial purpose or "why." Taking time for deep introspection can be instrumental. Reflect on the reasons you began a particular journey. Was it a childhood dream? A solution to a problem you deeply cared about?

By revisiting and reconnecting with your original intentions and motivations, you can reignite the spark that initiated your journey. Journaling, meditation, or even a simple quiet time can aid in this introspection.

2. Set Small, Achievable Goals:

Sometimes, the enormity of a goal or the vastness of a journey can feel overwhelming, leading to a reduction in drive. By breaking your objectives into smaller, more immediate tasks, you can create a series of achievable steps. Each completed task can act as a mini victory, providing a dopamine boost and reinvigorating your passion for the larger goal.

3. Surround Yourself with Positivity:

Your environment plays a pivotal role in influencing your state of mind. Surrounding yourself with positive, enthusiastic individuals who share similar goals or passions can be invigorating.

Their energy and perspective can provide fresh insights, motivation, and a renewed sense of purpose. Engaging in discussions, brainstorming sessions, or simply sharing experiences can offer a fresh perspective and rekindle passion.

4. Seek Inspiration:

Recharge your creative batteries by exposing yourself to new experiences and ideas. This could mean traveling to a new place, reading a book outside of your usual genres, attending workshops, or listening to inspirational talks. Fresh stimuli can provide novel insights, challenge your existing beliefs, and reignite curiosity and passion.

5. Embrace Change and Novelty:

Routine and monotony can often dampen enthusiasm. Introducing change, whether in your work processes, environment, or daily habits, can break the monotony.

Trying a new approach, rearranging your workspace, or even adopting a new hobby can introduce the novelty that stimulates enthusiasm and drive.

6. Take Constructive Breaks:

Burnout is a real threat to passion and drive. Recognizing when to step back and take a break is crucial. However, this doesn't mean idling away time.

Engage in activities that rejuvenate you, whether it's hiking, pursuing a hobby, or simply spending quality time with loved ones. Such constructive breaks can refresh your mind and provide a renewed sense of vigor.

7. Mentorship and Giving Back:

One profound way to rediscover passion is by mentoring or teaching others in your field. Imparting knowledge can remind you of the love you have for your craft.

Watching someone else grow and flourish due to your guidance can be incredibly fulfilling and can reignite your own passion and purpose.

Reigniting passion and drive are a deeply personal journey. What works for one may not work for another. However, these techniques offer a versatile toolkit that can be tailored to individual needs, ensuring sustained enthusiasm and drive in one's pursuits.

Inspirational Anecdotes to Keep the Flame Alive

The Story of Bethany Hamilton:

Bethany Hamilton was just a teenager when a shark attack changed her life forever, costing her an arm. But, instead of letting the incident define her, Bethany chose to define herself.

Within months, she was back on her surfboard, challenging the massive waves once again. Her indomitable spirit wasn't to prove anything to the world, but to herself, that she wouldn't be held back by circumstances.

Her story isn't just about her return to professional surfing, but about her embrace of life in its entirety, with all its ups and downs.

Bethany's journey shows us that sometimes, our greatest challenges can mold us into the best version of ourselves, reminding us never to let go of our passions, no matter the odds.

Thomas Edison's Persistent Experiments:

The invention of the light bulb wasn't a sudden 'aha' moment as some stories might lead you to believe. In reality, Thomas Edison endured thousands of failed attempts before he finally cracked the code.

After every setback, he famously remarked, "I have not failed. I've just found 10,000 ways that won't work."

Edison's relentless pursuit teaches us the significance of viewing failures not as the end but as learning opportunities.

His journey is a testament to the belief that consistent effort, coupled with an unwavering belief in oneself, can illuminate even the darkest corners of doubt.

J.K. Rowling's Rejections:

Before J.K. Rowling became a household name with her "Harry Potter" series, she faced numerous rejections from multiple publishers.

Living as a single mother, grappling with poverty, Rowling found solace in the magical world she was creating. Despite the discouragements, she held firm to her belief in the story, persisting until she finally saw her work in print.

Today, her books have not only achieved legendary status but have also inspired millions worldwide, teaching them about courage, friendship, and the transformative power of love.

Rowling's journey underscores the importance of believing in one's vision, even when faced with adversities or when the world fails to recognize its value.

Dashrath Manjhi's Mountainous Task:

In a remote village in India, Dashrath Manjhi took it upon himself to carve a path through a mountain using only a hammer and chisel.

The task seemed impossible to many, but Manjhi was driven by a personal tragedy: his wife had died due to the lack of a direct route to the nearest medical center.

It took him 22 years, but Manjhi eventually created a road 360 feet long, making the journey between neighboring towns significantly shorter and safer.

While Manjhi wasn't an engineer or a professional builder, his undying determination transformed an impassable terrain into a pathway of hope.

His story is a profound reminder that determination, coupled with a strong 'why', can move mountains, literally.

Each of these anecdotes illustrates the boundless potential within every individual. They remind us that with perseverance, belief, and a sprinkle of passion, one can overcome any challenge and keep the flame of hope and inspiration alive.

Chapter 10: Community and Its Role in Resilience

Throughout history, humans have sought solace in the company of others. From the earliest days when primitive men and women banded together for survival, to our complex societal structures today, the sense of community has been an integral part of our evolution.

It's not just a cultural or social phenomenon; it's an innate human need. In this digital age of connectivity, where one can have thousands of 'friends' yet feel profoundly alone, understanding the true essence of community and its pivotal role in resilience becomes even more crucial.

In the face of adversity, whether personal or collective, it's often the strength of community that becomes our lifeline. Be it the comforting words from a neighbor during times of grief, the collective efforts of a town recovering from a natural disaster, or global movements rallying for a shared cause, community is the bedrock upon which resilience is built.

This chapter delves deep into the fabric of community, exploring its transformative power and highlighting its significance in fostering resilience.

Through inspiring stories from around the globe, practical insights, and poignant reflections, we'll journey together to recognize the undeniable bond between community and resilience. It is a testament to the adage that while individuals can break, communities bend, adapt, and come back stronger.

Stories of Communities Overcoming Collective Challenges

Black Wall Street and the Tulsa Race Massacre:

In the early 20th century, the Greenwood District in Tulsa, Oklahoma, often referred to as "Black Wall Street", was a flourishing African-American community known for its thriving businesses and economic prowess.

However, in 1921, a racially motivated attack resulted in the destruction of this prosperous district, with many residents killed and businesses decimated.

Despite this horrific tragedy, the survivors of the Tulsa Race Massacre displayed exceptional resilience. In the years that followed, the community came together, pooling resources and relying on each other's strengths, to rebuild Greenwood.

Though it never regained its former glory, the sheer determination of the community serves as a testament to the power of collective effort.

The Irish Potato Famine and Emigration:

The mid-19th century saw Ireland grappling with a devastating potato blight that led to widespread famine. Over a million Irish individuals perished due to starvation and associated diseases, and an equivalent number sought refuge abroad.

The Irish diaspora, spread mainly across the U.S., Canada, and Australia, displayed a powerful collective spirit.

Irish communities abroad supported each other, setting up support systems, aiding new arrivals, and preserving their culture and traditions.

Through festivals, gatherings, and mutual aid societies, they not only overcame the socio-economic challenges in their new homes but also ensured that future generations remembered their origins and the trials their forebears faced.

Chernobyl Disaster and the Liquidators:

The 1986 Chernobyl nuclear disaster is one of the most catastrophic man-made disasters in history. Following the explosion, the immediate and long-term threat of radiation loomed large.

However, over 600,000 individuals, known as 'Liquidators', rallied to contain the damage. These brave souls, comprising plant workers, firefighters, engineers, and soldiers, took on immense personal risk to prevent further radioactive release.

They worked to put out fires, build containment structures, and clean the affected areas. The collective spirit of the Liquidators, fueled by a shared understanding of the gravity of the situation, was instrumental in averting a more extensive disaster. Their unity and determination remain a symbol of collective resilience in the face of unprecedented challenges.

The Aceh Tsunami and Reconstruction:

In December 2004, the province of Aceh in Indonesia bore the brunt of one of the deadliest tsunamis in history. Triggered by an undersea earthquake, massive waves battered the coast, claiming over 160,000 lives in Aceh alone.

The scale of destruction was staggering, with entire towns wiped out and infrastructure severely damaged. However, what followed was a remarkable story of community resilience.

The Acehnese, along with national and international aid, embarked on a massive reconstruction effort. Communities were rebuilt from the ground up, with residents collaborating to re-establish schools, homes, and local businesses.

Collective efforts, grounded in a shared sense of loss and hope, transformed Aceh from a disaster zone to a beacon of recovery and renewal.

These stories, among countless others, underscore the indomitable human spirit. When communities come together, driven by a shared purpose and mutual support, they can overcome even the most daunting challenges.

The Importance of Seeking Help and Building A Team

The Importance of Seeking Help

In a society that often celebrates individual achievements and self-reliance, it's easy to fall into the trap of believing that seeking help is a sign of weakness. However, the opposite is true. Seeking help when faced with challenges is not only a sign of strength but also of wisdom.

History and contemporary experiences alike show that many of the world's most impactful successes are born from collaboration, consultation, and shared efforts.

Every individual, regardless of their capability or expertise, has limitations. There are areas where our knowledge might be lacking, situations we've never encountered, or emotions we don't know how to navigate.

Seeking guidance or assistance in these instances doesn't diminish our efforts; instead, it amplifies them. By acknowledging areas of uncertainty and reaching out for support, individuals can gather diverse perspectives, gain new insights, and devise more effective strategies to overcome obstacles.

Furthermore, reaching out for help can also serve as a protective factor for mental well-being. Isolation and the feeling of being overwhelmed are potent stressors. When we share our burdens, even if just by talking about them, they become more manageable.

In numerous instances, from entrepreneurship to personal endeavors, many have noted that it was a timely piece of advice, a shared resource, or simple encouragement from another that made the critical difference in their journey.

Building a Team

Building a team goes hand-in-hand with seeking help. While the former is about recognizing one's limitations, the latter is about leveraging collective strengths.

A well-assembled team brings together individuals with complementary skills, ensuring that the group can tackle a challenge from multiple angles.

Each member's unique experiences, expertise, and approach enrich the group's dynamics, making the team more versatile and adaptable.

The process of team building is more than just grouping individuals together. It's about fostering trust, encouraging open communication, and establishing a shared vision.

When these elements are in place, teams can achieve far more than the sum of their individual contributions.

The innovation born from team brainstorming sessions, the problem-solving capacity when multiple minds work in tandem, and the sheer drive generated by mutual motivation are all testaments to the power of collective effort.

Moreover, teams provide a sense of belonging, a crucial factor for human well-being. Being part of a team can serve as a buffer against external pressures, provide emotional support during trying times, and celebrate successes in a way that magnifies the joy of achievement.

History has repeatedly shown us that while individual brilliance is remarkable, collective effort is transformative. From moon landings to revolutionary social changes, the power of teams is undeniable.

In essence, both seeking help and building a team underscore the fundamental human truth: we are inherently social beings, wired for connection, collaboration, and community.

By embracing these aspects, we not only bolster our chances of success but also enrich our journey with shared experiences and relationships.

Strategies to Build and Nurture A Supportive Community

1. Clearly Define the Community's Purpose and Values:

Every successful community starts with a clear sense of purpose. Whether it's a group focused on a specific hobby, professional networking, or personal growth, understanding and defining the "why" behind the community gives members a reason to join and remain engaged. Along with purpose, it's equally vital to set forth the community's core values.

These values become the guiding principles that dictate behavior, interactions, and decisions within the group. When members understand and resonate with both the purpose and values, they are more likely to contribute positively and actively.

2. Create Inclusive and Safe Spaces:

A supportive community thrives on inclusivity. It's crucial to ensure that everyone, regardless of their background, experience, or perspective, feels welcomed and heard.

This means actively addressing and preventing discrimination, harassment, and other negative behaviors. Establishing community guidelines and emphasizing a zero-tolerance policy for any form of bigotry or bullying can create a foundation of trust and safety.

Additionally, offer platforms or avenues where members can share their concerns confidentially and ensure that these concerns are addressed promptly.

3. Encourage Member Participation and Ownership:

Engagement is the lifeblood of any community. Actively involve members by creating avenues for them to contribute, be it through organizing events, leading discussions, or sharing resources.

When members take on roles or responsibilities, it fosters a sense of ownership and commitment to the community's success. Platforms like discussion boards, community polls, or collaborative projects can be instrumental in spurring active participation.

4. Regularly Organize Events and Gatherings:

Whether virtual or physical, events can be a powerful tool to strengthen bonds among community members. These can range from workshops, webinars, and seminars to informal meet-ups, social outings, or retreats. Such gatherings not only facilitate learning but also enable members to form personal connections, share experiences, and collaborate on shared interests or projects.

5. Foster Open Communication:

Open and transparent communication sets the tone for mutual respect and understanding within a community. Encourage members to voice their opinions, ask questions, and share feedback.

Platforms like community forums, chat groups, or regular town-hall meetings can facilitate open dialogues. Additionally, community leaders or moderators should be approachable and proactive in addressing any issues or concerns raised by members.

6. Celebrate Successes and Acknowledge Contributions:

Recognizing and celebrating the achievements of community members can create a positive and motivating environment. Whether it's a member's personal accomplishment, a successful community event, or the contribution of volunteers, acknowledging these efforts instils pride and encourages further participation. This could be done through regular shout-outs, awards, or even simple thank-you notes.

7. Continuously Evolve and Adapt:

No community remains static. As members come and go and the external environment changes, the community's needs and dynamics will shift. Regularly solicit feedback, be open to making necessary changes, and adapt to the evolving needs and aspirations of the community.

This could involve introducing new tools, changing communication strategies, or even revisiting the community's core objectives and values.

By implementing these strategies and maintaining a genuine commitment to the well-being and growth of its members, community leaders can successfully build and nurture a thriving, supportive community.

Chapter 11: Preparing for Future Challenges

Life is often described as a journey, a winding path filled with hills to climb, rivers to cross, and obstacles to navigate. While the earlier chapters have equipped you with the tools, strategies, and resilience techniques employed by some of the world's most successful individuals, this chapter serves a slightly different yet essential purpose. It aims to help you become future-ready.

We've dissected the elements of resilience, drawn lessons from towering figures of history and modernity, and provided you with actionable strategies. Now, we must address a crucial question: How do you prepare for challenges that lie ahead, especially the ones that are unforeseen?

In this chapter, we delve into the art of foresight, not fortune-telling but planning with wisdom. By forecasting potential personal and societal challenges, we can not only mitigate their impact but often transform them into stepping stones for further growth.

We'll explore techniques to prepare mentally, emotionally, and even physically for what lies ahead. Consider this chapter as your guide to constructing a 'resilience toolkit' that evolves with you, enabling you to face future challenges head-on and with confidence.

As the saying goes, "Failing to prepare is preparing to fail." After completing this chapter, you'll be armed with a framework to ensure that your future self will look back and thank you for the groundwork you laid today. So, let's journey into the future and carve a path that turns challenges into opportunities for growth and fulfillment.

By the end of this chapter, you'll not only be well-versed in overcoming obstacles but also become proficient in anticipating them. In doing so, you'll find that resilience isn't just a reactive skill, but a proactive one that influences the quality of your life for years to come.

Are you ready? Let's turn the page and step into the future, fortified with the wisdom and resilience techniques that will make all the difference.

Forecasting Potential Personal and Societal Challenges

Forecasting Personal Challenges:

The trajectory of an individual's life, though unique, often follows patterns and cycles. Some challenges are almost universal due to life stages, such as the struggles faced during adolescence, midlife crises, or the physical and mental challenges in our senior years.

Additionally, based on one's current lifestyle, health habits, and personal relationships, one can anticipate potential future problems.

For instance, someone working in a high-stress job might foresee burnout if they don't take proactive measures. Similarly, neglecting personal relationships might lead to feelings of isolation or estrangement in the future.

Personal financial decisions made today, such as excessive spending or not saving for retirement, can lead to economic hardships.

Forecasting these challenges involves a deep self-awareness, understanding one's vulnerabilities, and sometimes seeking insights from counselling or therapy to identify and mitigate potential future issues.

Forecasting Societal Challenges:

On a broader scale, societal challenges can be forecasted by studying current global trends, technological advancements, and socio-political shifts.

Historically, major societal changes have often been preceded by smaller indications, which, if noticed and analyzed, can hint at larger transformations or challenges to come.

For instance, climate change, which has been a point of discussion for several decades, is now manifesting in more frequent extreme weather events, rising sea levels, and other ecological challenges.

Economists and environmentalists had been forecasting these events, and now societies worldwide are grappling with their realities and consequences.

Another example is the realm of technology and digitalization. As we've embraced a more digital lifestyle, issues surrounding data privacy, cybersecurity threats, and even the societal implications of artificial intelligence have come to the forefront.

These challenges were forecasted by tech visionaries and experts who observed the rapid rate of tech integration in our daily lives.

Furthermore, demographic shifts, such as aging populations in many developed countries, forecast challenges related to healthcare, pensions, and a potential lack of a young workforce. Conversely, countries with booming young populations might face employment and educational challenges.

Economic patterns, political tensions, and even cultural shifts also offer forecasts about potential societal challenges. For example, the rise of populist movements worldwide indicates a growing discontent with established systems and can forecast societal disruptions or transformations.

In essence, forecasting societal challenges requires a multidisciplinary approach. It involves staying informed, understanding interconnections, and being receptive to patterns and changes, no matter how subtle they might appear initially.

By anticipating these challenges, both on a personal and societal level, individuals and communities can better prepare, adapt, and even innovate solutions to navigate them effectively.

Techniques to Prepare Mentally, Emotionally, And Physically

Mentally:

Mental preparation is vital for handling challenges and adapting to unforeseen situations. With the right mindset, one can face difficulties head-on and find innovative solutions.

- **Education and Continuous Learning:**
  1. Engage in regular reading, webinars, or workshops on topics relevant to one's goals or challenges.
  2. Take courses that challenge your thinking or broaden your horizons.
  3. Stay updated with industry or field-specific news to anticipate challenges.

- **Mindfulness and Meditation:**
  1. Practice regular meditation to enhance focus, clarity, and calmness.
  2. Engage in mindfulness exercises to stay present and prevent overwhelm.
  3. Use guided visualizations to mentally rehearse challenging situations and find solutions.

- **Positive Affirmations:**
  1. Begin the day with positive affirmations to set a constructive tone.
  2. Use affirmations to counter negative self-talk and reinforce belief in one's capabilities.
  3. Create a personal mantra to return to during moments of doubt or stress.

Emotionally:

Emotional resilience ensures that one remains stable and can bounce back from setbacks. A healthy emotional state enables better decision-making and fosters positive relationships.

- **Emotional Regulation Techniques:**
1. Engage in deep breathing exercises to calm heightened emotions.
2. Use the "STOP" method: Stop, take a breath, observe your feelings, Proceed with awareness.
3. Journal feelings regularly to process and understand them better.

- **Building a Support System:**
1. Cultivate and maintain relationships with friends, family, or mentors who offer emotional support.
2. Join support groups or communities with shared experiences or challenges.
3. Seek professional therapy or counselling for deeper emotional challenges.

- **Setting Boundaries:**
1. Recognize and articulate personal limits in professional and personal situations.
2. Schedule regular self-care routines to recharge emotionally.
3. Learn to say "no" when necessary to protect emotional well-being.

Physically:

A strong and healthy body can be a cornerstone for facing challenges. Physical preparation isn't just about strength but also about endurance, flexibility, and overall well-being.

- **Regular Exercise:**
  1. Engage in a balanced routine that includes cardiovascular, strength, and flexibility training.
  2. Set aside dedicated time daily or several times a week to engage in physical activity.
  3. Explore diverse forms of exercise like yoga, Pilates, or martial arts to enhance different aspects of physical health.

- **Nutrition:**
  1. Maintain a balanced diet rich in whole foods, lean proteins, and healthy fats.
  2. Avoid excessive consumption of processed foods, sugars, and excessive caffeine.
  3. Stay hydrated with water, and consider supplements if needed and after consulting with a health professional.

- **Rest and Recovery:**
  1. Ensure 7-9 hours of sleep each night for optimal physical recovery and cognitive function.
  2. Engage in relaxation techniques such as deep breathing, massages, or warm baths.
  3. Take breaks during the day, especially if one's work is sedentary, to stretch and move around.

By integrating these techniques, one can holistically prepare for challenges and maintain a state of readiness for life's various obstacles.

Building A 'Resilience Toolkit' For the Future

In a rapidly changing world, where the only certainty is uncertainty, cultivating resilience is paramount. But resilience isn't just a mindset; it's an active process that involves preparation, understanding, and an arsenal of tools ready for deployment. This is where the concept of a 'resilience toolkit' comes into play.

A resilience toolkit is a collection of resources, strategies, and practices tailored to help individuals cope, adapt, and thrive in the face of adversity. It's akin to having a first-aid kit for mental and emotional well-being, filled with tools that are prepped and ready to handle the unpredictable challenges of life.

Constructing this toolkit requires thoughtful introspection, learning from past experiences, and actively seeking out new tools that resonate with one's personal journey.

To start, the foundation of any resilience toolkit is self-awareness. Being deeply attuned to one's emotions, strengths, weaknesses, triggers, and coping mechanisms forms the bedrock of resilience. Tools like journaling, mindfulness meditation, and regular self-reflection exercises can assist in enhancing this self-awareness.

Next, is the tool of adaptability. In the age of digital disruption and global shifts, the ability to adapt is crucial. This involves developing a growth mindset, where challenges are viewed not as insurmountable barriers but as opportunities for learning and growth.

This mindset can be fostered through exposure to diverse situations, continuous learning, and embracing change, even when it feels uncomfortable.

Social support systems are another invaluable component. Human beings are inherently social creatures, and having a network of support during times of distress can be a game-changer. This doesn't just refer to friends and family, but also to mentors, therapists, and peer groups. Actively nurturing these relationships, seeking out communities that share similar values, and not being afraid to lean on them during trying times are essential strategies.

Another tool involves having a 'future-oriented perspective'. This means always having a forward-looking view, setting goals, and visualizing a better future. Even during the most challenging times, focusing on a positive, achievable future can provide the motivation needed to push through. Techniques such as vision boarding, setting SMART goals, and positive affirmation practices can assist in maintaining this perspective.

Finally, a continuous commitment to self-improvement and learning completes the toolkit. This involves constantly updating and refining the tools based on new experiences, insights, and challenges faced. Just like a craftsman sharpens their tools regularly, the resilience toolkit requires constant maintenance and upgrading.

In conclusion, building a resilience toolkit for the future is a proactive approach to mental and emotional well-being. It's a recognition that challenges will come, but with the right tools at one's disposal, they can not only be faced but conquered with grace, strength, and confidence.

Conclusion

Congratulations on making it to this point in your journey of understanding resilience and overcoming obstacles. You've traversed through the intricate landscape of challenges, seen through the eyes of historical figures and modern-day titans, and delved into strategies that can turn setbacks into stepping stones.

Just as every story has an ending, every obstacle has a resolution, and every challenge contains the seeds of opportunity. As we close this book, it's vital to revisit the essence of what we've discussed, distilled into actionable insights you can apply in your own life.

In this concluding chapter, we will summarize the key lessons learned and the techniques acquired, helping you to integrate them into a personalized 'resilience toolkit.' Think of this as your compass, a guide you can rely on when navigating the turbulent seas of life's challenges.

We'll also explore what it means to carry forward this newfound knowledge and how to keep building on it. Because the process of overcoming obstacles is a lifelong journey, and your story of resilience is an ongoing narrative. Let's wrap up by solidifying your next steps in this enduring voyage towards resilience and success.

The Ongoing Journey of Resilience

Resilience is not a fixed trait or a one-time accomplishment; rather, it's a dynamic process, a continuous journey that unfolds throughout our lives. It's akin to a muscle that needs consistent training, honing, and adapting, especially as the challenges we face evolve over time.

Every individual's life is punctuated by a myriad of events, some joyous, some tragic, some seemingly insurmountable. With each of these events, there is an opportunity to practice and cultivate resilience, ensuring we are better prepared for the next obstacle.

At its core, resilience is about adaptation. It's the capacity to bounce back from adversities, yes, but it's also about growing from them. It's about learning, understanding, and integrating experiences, whether they're positive or negative. Over time, as we encounter a diverse array of challenges, our toolbox of coping mechanisms expands.

We learn which strategies work best for us and which ones don't. This personal evolution means that resilience is not static; it changes as we do. A strategy that might have worked for us in our youth may not be as effective in our later years, pushing us to develop new methods of coping and growing.

Furthermore, the journey of resilience is deeply personal, yet it's also profoundly communal. Our resilience is often influenced by the communities we're part of, the shared stories we hear, and the collective wisdom we inherit. Humans, by nature, are social beings.

We derive strength from shared experiences, from knowing that others too have faced tribulations and have not only survived but thrived. This shared narrative creates a tapestry of resilience, where each individual's story is a thread that strengthens the collective fabric.

In embracing the ongoing nature of resilience, it's crucial to acknowledge that setbacks are a part of this journey. There will be moments of doubt, instances where we feel our resilience wane. However, it's in these moments that the true essence of resilience shines through.

It's not about avoiding difficulties but navigating through them, using them as catalysts for growth. With each hurdle overcome, the journey of resilience progresses, paving the way for not only personal transformation but also the upliftment of communities and societies at large.

As life continues its unpredictable dance, it's heartening to know that our capacity for resilience is ever-evolving. With each challenge faced, with each story shared, and with each lesson learned, we further our journey, fortifying ourselves and our communities for the future. In this ever-changing world, resilience remains our steadfast companion, guiding us through both calm and stormy seas.

Embrace Challenges and See Them as Opportunities

Embracing Challenges:

Life is inherently full of challenges. From the mundane day-to-day tasks to the larger, more intimidating hurdles, each one offers a chance to learn, grow, and evolve. Many people naturally shy away from challenges due to a fear of failure, potential ridicule, or the uncertainty that these challenges bring. However, adopting a mindset that views these challenges not as setbacks but as catalysts for growth can completely alter one's life trajectory.

To truly embrace a challenge means to lean into the discomfort it might bring. It's easy to remain in the cozy cocoon of the familiar, but breaking out of one's comfort zone is where real growth happens. Each challenge, irrespective of its outcome, provides invaluable lessons. Even in failure, there is a plethora of wisdom to be gained. It's a testament to one's courage, a training ground for adaptability, and a platform to sharpen skills.

Seeing Challenges as Opportunities:

Every challenge is, in essence, a door. Behind that door lie potential opportunities that we might never have encountered had we not taken on the challenge in the first place. The adage, "When one door closes, another opens," rings true here. For instance, an artist might face rejection from multiple galleries, but this challenge can push them to explore alternative platforms or mediums, leading them to discover a more authentic voice or a broader audience.

Furthermore, challenges force us to dig deep, tapping into reservoirs of determination, creativity, and resilience we might not have known existed. They push us to think outside the box, to innovate, and to adapt. Each of these skills is invaluable and once honed, opens up countless opportunities in personal and professional spheres.

Moreover, challenges enrich our character. Overcoming them breeds confidence, empathy (as we understand others' struggles better), and a deep-seated sense of achievement. These attributes not only equip us to tackle future challenges head-on but also make us more valuable in team settings, as mentors, and in leadership roles.

In the grand tapestry of life, challenges are not mere threads of adversity but vibrant strokes of color, adding depth, character, and beauty to the overall picture. It's only by viewing challenges as opportunities that we can fully appreciate their potential to transform our lives. Whether it's a personal growth spurt, a newfound skill, or an unexpected path, the opportunities that arise from challenges are the universe's way of pushing us towards our best selves.

To Continue Growing, Learning, and Building Resilience

Life, in all its unpredictability, is not about reaching a plateau of perpetual happiness or a state of permanent equilibrium. It's about the journey, the ebbs and flows, the challenges met, and the lessons learned.

Each one of us, regardless of our backgrounds or circumstances, will encounter obstacles that test our mettle, shake our foundations, and sometimes, bring us to our knees. But herein lies our shared human potential: the capacity to rise, to learn, and to grow stronger with each challenge. This book is not just a testament to that potential, but a fervent call to action.

Growth is an ongoing process, not a destination. It is the conscious effort to expand our horizons, to step out of our comfort zones, and to embrace the unknown. It requires a hunger for knowledge and a thirst for experiences that stretch our boundaries and shatter our preconceptions.

And just as a muscle grows through strain and recovery, our personal growth is catalyzed by the challenges we face and our reactions to them. It is crucial to remind ourselves that growth is a choice, one we must make daily.

Learning, too, is a ceaseless journey. In an ever-evolving world, yesterday's knowledge might be obsolete today, and today's wisdom might be outdated tomorrow. The landscapes of technology, society, and personal relations are in constant flux. To navigate this dynamic world, continuous learning is not just beneficial, it's imperative.

Be it formal education, self-guided reading, or experiential lessons, every nugget of knowledge we acquire is a tool, a weapon, a shield against ignorance. Embrace learning as a lifelong partner, for it illuminates the path forward, no matter how dark the night.

Lastly, building resilience is the cornerstone of facing life's storms with grace and tenacity. Resilience is not a trait we're born with but a skill we develop. Like a blacksmith tempers steel, life tempers us with challenges.

Each adversity we face, each obstacle we overcome, reinforces our spirit, making us more resilient for future battles. It's an iterative process; with each challenge faced, our resilience muscle gets stronger, preparing us for the next. And remember, resilience is not just about bouncing back, but bouncing forward, evolving with each setback, and emerging better than before.

In conclusion, this isn't a mere ending, but a beginning. It's an invitation to you, the reader, to take the reins of your life firmly in hand. To decide, here and now, to commit to a life of continuous growth, unending learning, and the relentless pursuit of resilience.

Because in this journey of life, the true victory is not in avoiding the storm, but in dancing in the rain, and emerging, drenched but undaunted, ready for the next challenge. Rise to this call, for a brighter, stronger, and more resilient tomorrow awaits.

Appendices

Glossary of Terms

Affirmations: Positive statements that can help you challenge and overcome self-sabotaging and negative thoughts.

Community: A group of individuals who share a commonality, which can be values, goals, interests, or experiences.

Emotional Intelligence (EI): The capacity to understand and manage your emotions, as well as to understand and influence the emotions of others.

External Obstacles: Challenges that arise outside of oneself, including environmental factors, societal pressures, and events beyond one's control.

Fixed Mindset: A belief that abilities and talents are static and cannot be developed or improved upon.

Growth Mindset: The belief that abilities and talents can be developed over time through dedication, hard work, and feedback.

Internal Obstacles: Challenges that arise from within, such as personal fears, doubts, or limiting beliefs.

Journaling: The practice of keeping a diary or journal to record one's thoughts, feelings, and experiences.

Mindfulness: A mental state achieved by focusing one's awareness on the present moment, while calmly acknowledging and accepting one's feelings, thoughts, and bodily sensations.

Mentor: An individual who offers guidance, support, and expertise to a less experienced person.

Perspective: A particular way of viewing situations, facts, and ideas, often shaped by personal experiences, upbringing, and beliefs.

Purpose: A person's sense of resolve or determination; a strong intention or aim.

Resilience: The capacity to recover quickly from difficulties; the ability to spring back into shape, both mentally and emotionally.

Self-Care: The practice of taking action to preserve or improve one's own health, well-being, and happiness.

Support System: A network of individuals, including family, friends, peers, and mentors, who provide emotional, practical, and informational support.

Vision Board: A visual representation of one's goals, dreams, and aspirations, usually created with a collection of images and words on a board or digital platform.